Jeff Gall

Walking—The Complete Book

ROSWELL REGIONAL LIBRARY

Jeff Galloway

Walking

The Complete Book

MEYER
& MEYER
SPORT

British Library Cataloguing in Publication Data
A catalogue record for this book is available from the British Library

Jeff Galloway – Walking—The Complete Book
Oxford: Meyer & Meyer Sport (UK) Ltd., 2006
ISBN 10: 1-84126-170-X
ISBN 13: 978-1-84126-170-6

All rights reserved, especially the right to copy and distribute,
including the translation rights. No part of this work may be reproduced—
including by photocopy, microfilm or any other means—
processed, stored electronically, copied or distributed in any form whatsoever
without the written permission of the publisher.

© 2006 by Meyer & Meyer Sport (UK) Ltd.
Aachen, Adelaide, Auckland, Budapest, Graz, Johannesburg,
New York, Olten (CH), Oxford, Singapore, Toronto
 Member of the World
Sports Publishers' Association (WSPA)
www.w-s-p-a.org
Printed and bound by: TZ Verlag, Germany
ISBN 10: 1-84126-170-X
ISBN 13: 978-1-84126-170-6
E-Mail: verlag@m-m-sports.com
www.m-m-sports.com

CONTENTS

WALKING IS FOR EVERYONE!

In my lifetime, I have helped more than 150,000 people learn to enjoy exercise and improve their quality of life. It has become clear to me that almost anyone can become an active walker without aches and pains. All you need to start this process is the desire to feel better, and the willingness to spend 3 half-hours a week gently moving your feet and legs. As you embrace the process of improvement, you will enjoy the glow of self- confidence and accomplishment. You are becoming a physical athlete.

When you cover a certain amount of distance on foot, you receive a unique sense of satisfaction which brings us back to our roots. According to the experts, primitive human ancestors defined and nurtured uniquely human traits during constant migrations. So I imagine that the "good tiredness" of the last mile of our walk makes one feel about the same as our ancestors more than one million years ago. This is the same process experienced by athletes as they train to become the best they can be.

Walking regularly makes you feel better, inserting energy into your life. It's convenient—you can walk from almost anywhere, on any day of the week. While you may need to alternate walk days and rest during the first few weeks, in a year most walkers can enjoy a walk every day. Some will want to try some short running segments, and the last chapter will tell you how to do this.

The purpose of this book is to connect you most directly with the benefits of walking. A primary goal is to help you become the captain of your exercise ship, and assume control over your nutrition and mental attitude while you eliminate aches and pains. If you stay on the conservative side, you will enrich your life every day you walk.

Whether you want to enjoy the glow of a neighborhood walk a few days a week, or take on the challenge of longer walks—5K, 10K, half marathon or marathon—the tools and information are in this book. Everything is better when you learn to enjoy each exercise session.

The material below is offered as advice, from one exerciser to another, fine-tuned after working with tens of thousands of exercisers like you, over more than 30 years. It is not meant to be medical consultation or scientific fact. For more information in these areas, see a physician or research the medical journals. But above all, laugh and enjoy your walking journey. It can change your life!

Jeff Galloway

BORN TO
WALK

Our ancestors managed to survive during the bleak and primitive beginnings of mankind because they possessed the intelligence to make tools and develop successful hunting strategies. They had to compete for food with other species who were both stronger and faster, and therefore had to cover long distances each day. Moving from one food supply to the next, day in and day out, became a never-ending quest to endure. By sheer necessity, their bodies physically adapted to "go the distance." In addition to their food, they received a variety of psychological and spiritual rewards.

So, in the eyes of many experts, mankind evolved because he was a long distance animal—and walking is at the core of our being. Other specialists in primitive man believe that the covering of thousands of miles every year in small groups forced the development of human traits of cooperation and mutual support. The data is continuing to show that we were born to walk.

Personal rewards

While the physical rewards described later are substantial, most long-time walkers acknowledge that the psychological ones are unique and more powerful. Here are a few of them:

Nature's pain killers

Hormones called endorphins serve as natural pain killers, and they have a positive psychological effect, producing a boost that lasts for hours after a good walk. Repeated use of the muscles, tendons, etc. causes internal monitors to sense there will be pain, and initiate endorphin production to manage it. Many of the good, relaxing, positive attitude effects of a walk come from these natural drugs...which are totally legal.

An attitude adjustment that injects vitality

After a walk, you will feel better, mentally and physically. Finishing a walk on a day when you had to push yourself out the door gives you a sense of victory. You feel more alive, better than normal, for several hours if not all day. A walk of 20 minutes or more almost always improves the way you feel about yourself and the world—with the energy to enjoy the rest of the day.

A sense of achievement

Moving ourselves on foot gives one a genuine sense of accomplishment. When your feet and muscles "conquer" several miles, you receive an authentic satisfaction based upon real work. This is one of the simple but satisfying rewards that have been passed on by our primitive ancestors. Bottom line is that we feel better about ourselves when we have covered some distance on that day.

There is even more enhanced self esteem in pushing back your current endurance level. As you keep going further on long walks, you feel an inner glow not experienced in other activities. In this book are training programs which can lead you to finish distances including a 26.2 mile marathon.

The marathon has become a major lifestyle achievement for many people. In fact, only one-tenth of one percent of the population finish one of these 26 mile events each year.

Conservative training using my walk-shuffle method, allows almost anyone to cross the finish line without pain. The sense of achievement from finishing this (or any event that is a challenge for you) almost always changes people for the better, and the change in lifestyle can last a lifetime.

Tapping into the right brain

Your intuition or gut instinct is engaged when you shift into the brain's right hemisphere. As you walk at a pace within your capabilities, you return to some primitive areas up there which have subconscious judgement capabilities and other powers we don't usually use.

I've conditioned my right brain to entertain me. I often start with a current problem or incident I'm trying to resolve. Ten minutes of forward movement later, the right brain has often taken a portion of the original thought and mixed in a personality of someone saying the words. After about 10 more minutes there is so much mixing of images and thoughts and associated mixed images that I have to laugh. Laughing is a right brain activity, and so is the series of images. This prompts the right brain to send me a mix of various images—some real and some very abstract—often without any connection to anything that came before. And on a few workouts each year, the solution to the original problem just drops out, into a conscious thought. But even when it doesn't, the right brain has entertained me for miles.

Less fatigure, more energy

When beginners start walking they expect to be more tired during the day. The vast majority, however, discover an unexpected opposite effect. A walk in the morning gives a boost of energy to mind and body for the day. You are activated, with a good attitude to deal with problems, and bounce back. Those who walk during lunch hour, when they used to work through lunch, find that they are more productive on the days they walk. Some say the scheduled walk forces them to plan better. Others describe how the mental boost and relaxation improves the quantity and quality of their work. Many say both are true—and more.

Newer, better friendships

For thousands of generations, humans have walked together. During these journeys experts believe many positive team-building and caring traits were developed: sharing trust, relying upon one another, and pulling one another through difficult times. These primitive instincts are revisited in almost any walk with another person or a group. I encourage you to find a group or individual that walks at your pace or slower.

Even when walking with one other person, you'll find yourself communicating feelings and emotions you wouldn't share when sitting down to a cozy lunch. After about 20 minutes of walking, under the influence of the right brain, you can bond more closely to your walking friends than to many family members who don't understand what exercise means to you.

Holding back the years

I regularly see walkers who don't look their age. When I look closely, the face and skin may give a general indication, but the vitality, mental energy, and good attitude would indicate an person that is 1-2 decades younger.

Why is this? In the act of extending your endurance, walkers are more likely to maintain a positive mental state. By injecting themselves with endorphins, they are more relaxed and confident. By using their muscles regularly and infusing them with oxygen on the walk, these people in their 70's, 80's and 90's feel good, have a healthy glow about them, and are physically able to do almost anything they did in their 40's.

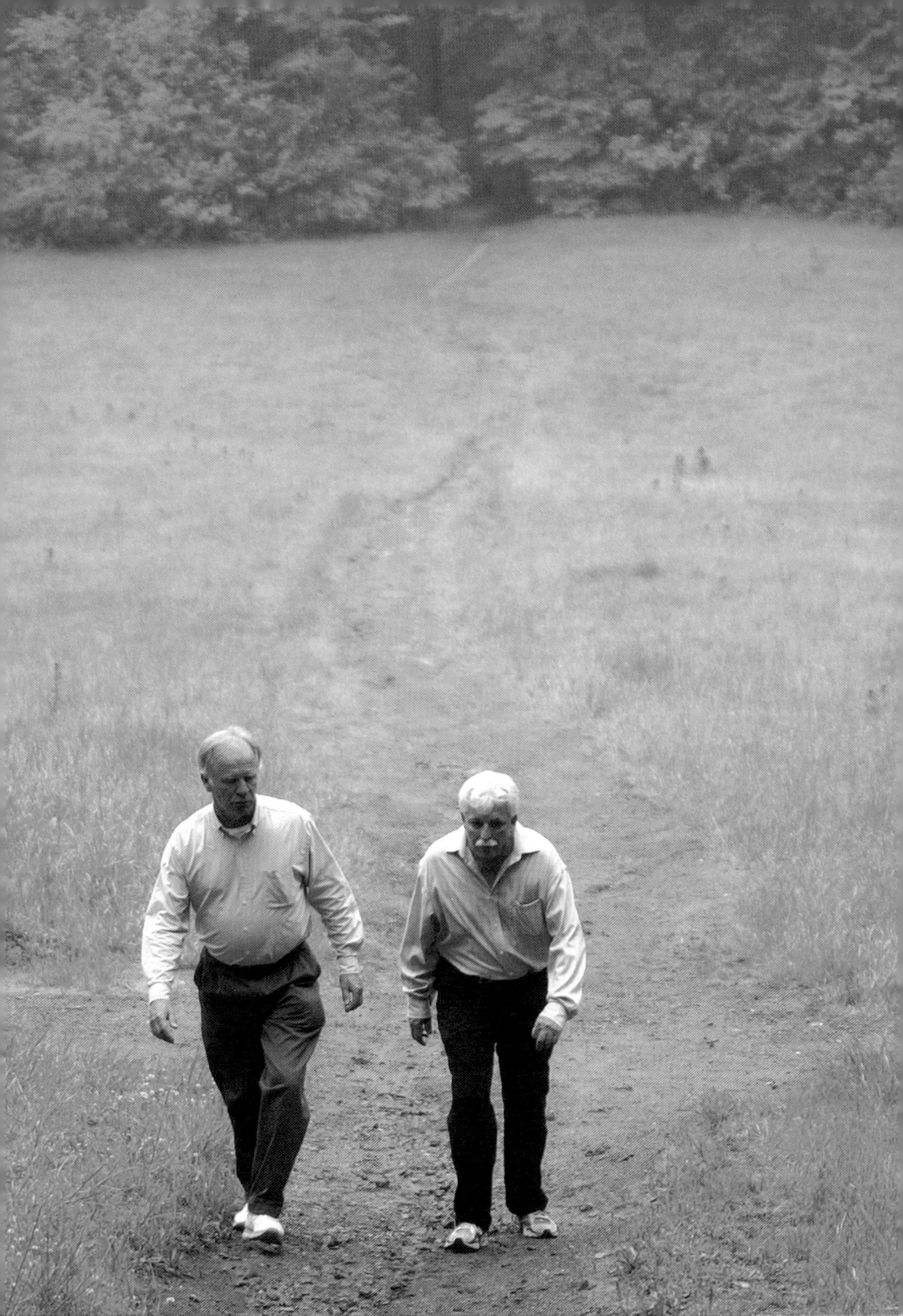

A sense of empowerment

The most important goal of this book is to help you move into the rewards of exercising more directly and easily. You can use this chapter to push you out the door on those days when gravity seems to be greater. Think about the good mental feelings after your walk and you'll have a "carrot on a stick" to keep you going when you want to quit. There will be times when you'll need to apply a reward or two as a psychological salve when overall motivation goes down on the hopefully few days when the inertia deck seems to be stacked against you.

The information and suggestions inside have been forged over more than 30 years of working with beginners, instructing and receiving feedback from more than 150,000 of them who have become regular exercisers. If you take charge over your walking life you can enjoy the many rewards while avoiding the aches and pains.

- You are pulling from resources that are inside you
- You find yourself becoming more intuitive as the right brain kicks in
- You feel the confidence to grapple with problems that formerly seemed insurmountable
- You find that you have more internal strength and creativity than you thought
- This enhanced feeling of energy and empowerment carries on to other areas of life.

Whatever time you have on earth, as a regular exerciser you'll have an opportunity to enjoy it to the fullest.

HOW WALKING GETS US "IN SHAPE"

Humans are designed to improve their fitness and endurance

When we regularly perform endurance exercise, many positive changes occur inside us. I believe that this is due to the way our ancient ancestors adapted our bodies to walk and run for long distances. Assuming, then that our physical design and purpose is long distance forward motion activity, it's no surprise that we feel so good when we do it—we are going back to our roots.

Is our body lazy?

Maybe this is too strong a statement. Let's say our bodies want to conserve resources by doing the smallest amount of work possible. If we are sedentary and never exercise, the heart slowly loses its efficiency, deposits build up in the arteries, and the lungs become less efficient because they don't need to be. Only when we put these important health components to gentle, regular tests (as in long walks) is the body forced to respond by improving in dozens of ways.

Teamwork

When called into action, the heart, lungs, muscles, tendons, central nerve transmission, brain and blood system are all programmed to work as a team. The right brain intuitively solves problems, manages resources, and steers us toward the many lasting health benefits resulting from endurance exercise.

Each muscle is like a factory composed of thousands of muscle cells which do the work. Unlike some factory workers, these are passionate and dedicated team members ready to work 24/7 to keep us moving—even when we push them to exhaustion over and over again. Walking, even in short amounts, done slowly, calls them into action, stimulates them to improve, and serves to mold them into a team.

Among other important functions, your leg muscles help to pump blood back to the heart. By gradually extending the length of your long walks, you produce very fit muscle cells in the legs. They get stronger and more efficient in moving blood in and pushing waste products through the system and back to the heart. Some cardiovascular experts who study the heart believe that the cumulative effect of endurance-trained leg muscle cells gives the heart a big boost by pumping blood back to it.

Why does long distance exercise keep the heart healthy?

Your heart is a muscle and responds positively to endurance exercise. The slight increase in heart rate, maintained during a gradually increasing long walk each week, keeps this most important muscle in shape. A strong and effective heart pumps blood more effectively, and not only when you exercise. Heart specialists say that this "fit" heart is more resistant to heart disease at all times.

But if your diet is full of artery-clogging foods, a strong heart will not make you immune to heart disease. Read the nutrition section of this book to find out more about which foods are high in saturated fat and trans fat.

The lungs

On our long walks, the muscles need oxygen to burn fat and exercise continuously. Through a series of long walks, our lungs are stimulated to improve oxygen absorption, and to more efficiently load up the red blood cells for continuous delivery of oxygen to exercising muscles.

Endorphins kill pain, make you feel good

Another important member of the team, the endorphins, manage muscle pain and provide a positive lift to the spirit.

What is endurance exercise?

The essence of endurance exercise is to go farther—to keep doing an exercise long enough so that the body must find more efficient ways of moving, of processing energy, sending blood, etc. For untrained muscles, a walk of 10 minutes will do this. As we push back this threshold, our first goal is to get to 3 sessions a week of 30 min each. For continuing progress, one of these could be a long one that pushes up to the current endurance limit or beyond (45 min, then 60 minutes, then whatever you want).

Long one once a week pushes back the endurance limits

plus

Two 30 minute sessions which maintain the adaptations gained on the long one

equals

You the endurance athlete

Stress + rest = improvement

When we walk a little farther than we've gone in the past month or so, the gentle stress breaks down the muscle cells, tendons, etc. This stimulates our bodies to rebuild, stronger than before, if you have enough rest afterward (usually 48 hours).

It all starts by gently stressing the system

When we exercise about every other day, our body becomes adapted to the speed and distance currently done. To improve endurance, we start by doing a walk that is slightly longer than we have been doing. As you exceed the current distance limit, tired muscle fibers keep working, beyond their capacity. The extra work of an additional half mile or mile may not be perceived during the longer walk, but often results in slightly more fatigue the next day: sore muscles, longer time needed to feel smooth when walking, and muscles that feel tired.

Looking inside the cell afterward, you'll see tears in the muscle cell membrane. The mitochondria (the energy processors inside the cell) are swollen. Glycogen (the energy supply needed for the first 15 minutes of exercise) is significantly reduced. There are waste products from exercise and even bits of muscle tissue and other residue from a hard effort. Sometimes, breaks in the blood vessels and arteries occur, with leakage of blood into the muscles. If you have only increased your distance by a mile or less (at a gentle pace for you) this damage can be repaired quickly. The damage actually stimulates improvements in the system.

The body rebuilds, stronger and better than before

Gentle overuse is a signal to the body that it must improve. The damage to the muscles caused by going slightly beyond capacity is not only repaired—the whole system is stimulated to improve in many ways. It becomes more efficient—able to handle more stress in the future.

If you have rested well, and look inside the cell again 2 days later, you'll see thicker cell membranes, which can handle more work without breaking down. The mitochondria have increased in size and number, so that they can process more energy next time. The damage to the blood system has been repaired. Waste has been removed. Over several months, after adapting to a continued series of small increases, more capilliaries (tiny fingers of the blood system) are produced, improving and expanding the delivery of oxygen and nutrients and providing a better withdrawal of waste products.

These are only some of the many adaptations that the incredible human body makes, at all levels, when we exercise: biomechanics, nervous system, strength, muscle efficiency and more. Psychological benefits go along with the physical ones. As your right brain senses that you are improving, you will glow with a relaxed feeling of self-confidence. As walkers improve conditioning they become more positive, internally sensing the empowerment that each is taking charge of their health, energy level and attitude. Mind, body and spirit are connecting up for great teamwork. These are only some of the reasons why walkers have been shown to be more positive people than they were before they regularly walked.

Quality rest is crucial: 48 hours between workouts

Without sufficient rest, the rebuilding will not proceed as quickly or as well as it could. I'm not talking about staying in bed all day after a strenuous walk. Quicker recovery is actually experienced if you gently walk around the rest of the day. The day after a longer walk, you can usually do gentle walks—as you do in everyday activities—and feel much better than if you remained sedentary.

The key to rebuilding stressed muscle cells is to avoid exercises that strenuously use the calf muscle (stair machines, step aerobics, spinning out of the saddle) for the 48 hour period after a hard walk. If you have other aches and pains from your individual "weak links" then don't do exercises that aggravate them further. As long as you are not continuing to stress the calf, most alternative exercises are fine.

"Beginning exercisers should treat each walk as a tough workout, and avoid leg tiring exercises for 48 hours."

If you don't have time on the days after walks to do any alternative exercise don't feel guilty. Cross- training is not necessary for walking improvement. Why do it? Well, it helps those who want to burn more fat. Also, many new walkers like the way they feel after a good walk and want to feel that way every day. Even walking 2 days in a row, in the beginning stages of a walking program, can produce significant damage and require much more recovery than an every-other day walk schedule. Once you find the cross-training mode that works best for you, you can enjoy the post-exercise glow every day.

Junk miles

Some beginners feel so good when they start a walking program that they "sneak in" a few miles on the days they should be resting. They often lie to themselves, assuming that this short distance isn't really tiring.

The problem is that these short walks, which don't improve your conditioning, don't give your muscles the rest needed for maximum recovery. They are called "junk miles." It's always better to stay with a 48 hour period between walks—the standard, proven recovery interval. With gentle increases, as noted in the training programs in this book, your body should rebound stronger than before, ready for a new challenge.

Regularity

To maintain the adaptations, you must regularly exercise every 2-3 days. Waiting longer than this, will cause a slight loss in the capacity you have been developing each day. The longer you wait beyond 3 days, the harder it will be to start up again. Staying regular with your exercise is the best policy.

"Muscle memory"

This is the process by which your neuro-muscular system remembers the patterns of muscle activity which you have done regularly, over an extended period of time. The longer you have been walking regularly, the easier it will be to start up when you've had a layoff. During your first month, for example, if you experience 3-4 days without walking (in a row), it will take a week to get back to the same level, and feel the same way. But if you have walked regularly for 6 months, and you can't walk for 3-4 days, you won't notice hardly any reduction in your conditioning as you start back.

Tip: Cramped for time? Just do 5 minutes

The main reason that beginners don't make progress is that they don't exercise regularly. Whatever it takes to keep you walking every other day—do it. Even if you only have 5-10 minutes, you will maintain most of the adaptations. The fact is that if you start out to do 5 minutes, you'll usually stay out for 10 or 15.

HOW TO GET STARTED

The objective for each day's walk is to feel good afterward—which gives you the desire to walk tomorrow. Once you take care of a few introductory steps listed in this chapter, you want to simplify the process of getting out the door each day. Walkers don't need facility or equipment— just comfortable shoes and clothes—but you'll discover that some are better than others. So...let's get started!

Walkers don't need ...

- A health club
- A team of other people
- A specific time of the day
- A specific uniform
- A piece of exercise equipment
- Lessons or a "pro" to supervise
- Competitive events

You are free to walk...

... by yourself

... from your home, office, kid's athletic field, etc.

... when you have time to do so, day or night

... wearing what you want to wear

... without phone, fax, beeper

The doctor's "green light"

Be sure to check with your doctor's office before you start walking. Just tell the doctor or head nurse that you plan to walk several times a week, then ask if there is anything that you need to be aware of (when to take prescribed medications, etc.) Almost every person will be given the green light. If your doctor recommends against walking, ask why. Since there are so few people who cannot walk if they

do so gently, I suggest that you get a second opinion if your doctor tells you "No." Certainly the tiny number of people who should not walk have good reasons. But the best medical advisor is one who wants you to get physical activity, and wants to help you get out there moving around because of the almost unlimited benefits.

Selecting a doctor

If your doctor is not very supportive of you exercising, ask the nurses in the office if there is another physician in the practice (or outside) who might be. Doctors who are advocates for fitness and encourage their patients to exercise are very often more positive and energetic.

The "grapevine" can help you find a doctor. Ask the staff at local running stores, running or walk club members, or long-term runners and walkers. They will usually know of several doctors in your town who support patients who exercise. You want a doctor who will support your walking habit, and serve as your "health coach"; someone who will work with you to boost health potential and avoid injury, sickness, and other health setbacks. Doctors have also told me that regular exercisers tend to have fewer bouts with sickness.

Your primary investment – Shoes! Typically between $65 and $100

Since shoes are the only real equipment needed for walking, most walkers wisely decide to spend a little time choosing a good shoe—usually a running shoe. The right shoe can make walking easier, while reducing blisters, foot fatigue and injuries. The right shoe can also increase your motivation to walk

Because there are so many different brands with many different models, shoe shopping can be confusing. The best advice….is to get the best advice. Going to a good running store, staffed by helpful and knowledgeable folks, can cut the time required and can usually lead you to a better shoe choice than you would find for yourself. While there are some shoes that are labeled "walking shoes," most walkers I've interviewed find that running shoes are more supportive, more comfortable, and fit better. The next section of this book will help to "walk" you through the process of choosing the right shoe.

Get a step counter—and shoot for 10,000 a day...then 11,000...

A good pedometer, or step counter, can make you a more active person. It will motivate and reward you for going the extra mile. This device that clips onto your belt or waist band, registers the number of steps that you take. You should wear it all day long—not just on your walks. You'll find yourself parking further away from your workplace, kid's athletic fields, etc. Seeing the total increase throughout the day is motivating and bestows an incentive to walk an extra time around the food store (to check the bargains), or around the soccer field (watching the kids practice), or to choose walking (vs sitting) while waiting for someone.

By adding steps to your day, you become a more active person, with more energy. During the first week, just collect the daily amounts and write the total on your calendar or journal. Whatever the average for the first 7 days, your mission is to increase that total by 1000 over the next week or two. Your first goal is 10,000 steps, but don't stop there.

All pedometers are not created equal. On our website you'll see some that have proven to be more reliable. The lower quality ones are inconsistent and often tell you that you walked a lot more than you really did. Expect to pay about $35 for a good one.

Clothing: put comfort first!

You don't have to have the latest techno-garments to walk. The "clothing thermometer" at the end of this book is a great guide. In summer, you want to wear light, cool clothing. During cold weather, layers are the best strategy. On most days loose fitting pants and a T-shirt are fine. On hot days, you'll be cooler with shorts and a tank top. As you get into walking, you will find various outfits that make you feel better and reduce or eliminate weather discomfort—even on the bad days. It is also OK to give yourself a fashionable outfit as a "reward" for staying with it regularly for several weeks.

Your training journal

The journal is such an important motivational component that I have written a chapter about it. By using it to plan ahead and then later, to review mistakes, you take a major degree of control over your exercise future. You'll find it reinforcing to write down what you did each day, and miss that reinforcement when you skip. Be sure to read the training journal chapter, and you'll see how it can be used to increase fat-burning, and gear up for strenuous hikes, etc.

Where to walk—safety first!

The best place to start is near your home or office—especially if there are sidewalks. First priority is safety. Pick a course that is away from car traffic, and is in an area where crime is unlikely. If you have several courses, you'll avoid boredom: variety can be very motivating.

Surface Considerations

With the selection of the right shoes for you and the correct amount of cushion, pavement should not give extra shock to the legs or body. A smooth surface, dirt or gravel path, is preferable to some walkers. But beware of an uneven surface especially if you have weak ankles or foot problems.

Find a walking buddy

Having someone to walk with can improve motivation and make the miles go by quickly. But don't walk with someone who is faster than you—unless he or she is fully comfortable slowing down to an easy pace that is comfortable for you. It is motivating to walk with someone who moves along at a comfortable pace so you can talk. Share stories, jokes, problems if you wish, and you'll bond together in a very positive way. The friendships forged on walks can be strong and long-lasting, if you're not huffing and puffing (or passing out) from trying to maintain a pace (or a stride length) that is a stretch for you.

Rewards for your progress

Being consistent is the most common reason for success, and regular rewards make you feel successful. If you're having motivation problems, rewards can help you get over a "hump," and make the first few weeks more interesting. Be sensitive to your motivation level and provide rewards before you start slacking off. Some of the items that have helped are comfortable shoes, clothes, a healthy snack afterward, etc.

Positive reinforcement works! Treating yourself to hot coffee after finishing a cold trek, a smoothie on a hot day, taking a cool dip in a pool, going out to a special restaurant after a longer walk—all of these can reinforce the good habit you are establishing. Of particular benefit is having a snack, within 30 minutes of the finish, that has about 200 calories, containing 80% carbohydrate and 20% protein. The products Accelerade and Endurox R4 are already formulated with this ratio for your convenience, and make good rewards for more strenuous walks that exceed 60 minutes.

Make an appointment (or two)

Schedule your walks about 2 weeks in advance, on your calendar or in your appointment book. Sure you can change if you have to. But by getting the walking "appointment" secure you will be able to plan for your time to walk, and make it happen. Pretend that this is an appointment with your boss, or your most important client, etc. Actually, you are your most important client when you are walking regularly.

Motivation – help getting out the door

There are two times when exercise motivation is often low: early in the morning and after work. In the motivation section there are rehearsals for each of these situations. You will find it much easier to be motivated once you experience a regular series of walks that make you feel good. Yes, when you walk at the right pace, with the right preparation, you feel better, can relate to others better, and have more energy to enjoy the rest of the day.

Treadmills work, too

Treadmills are now used for at least 50% of walks— particularly by those who have small children. It is a fact that treadmills tend to tell you that you have gone further or faster than you really have (but usually are not off by more than 10%).

But if you walk on treadmill for the number of minutes assigned, at the effort level you are used to (no huffing and puffing), you will get close enough to the training effect you wish. To ensure that you have enough distance for that day, feel free to add 10% to the goal distance on the treadmill monitor.

No need for chow first

Most walkers don't need to eat before walks that are less than 5 miles. But if you have diabetes or severe blood sugar problems, eating a snack an hour before the start can help. Many walkers feel better during a walk when they have enjoyed a cup of coffee about an hour before the start. Caffeine engages the central nervous system, which gets all of the systems needed for exercise up and running to capacity, very quickly.

If your blood sugar is low, which often occurs in the afternoon, it helps to have a snack of about 100-200 calories, composed of 80% carbohydrate and 20% protein— about 30 minutes before the start of your walk. The Accelerade product has been very successful in boosting blood sugar.

BUYING THE RIGHT SHOES

Even if you never plan to run a single step you should visit a technical running store. Of all the places you can go to buy shoes, you will tend to find the most experienced staff at these stores. To find the best store(s) in your area, ask several runners, particularly those who have run for 10 years or more. You want one that has a reputation for spending time with each customer in order to find a shoe that will best match the shape and function of the foot. Be prepared to spend at least 45 minutes in the store. Quality stores are often busy, and quality fitting takes time. But this is time well spent. Getting good advice can reduce or eliminate foot pain, blisters, etc.

Experienced running store staff can direct you toward shoes that give you a better fit and work better on your feet. I hear from exercisers every week who got a "great deal" on a pair of shoes which they now use for mowing the lawn because they didn't work on their feet. Good advice can help you avoid buying mistakes, and increase the chance that you will like the way your feet feel on every walk.

The best shoes for walkers are generally running shoes

While there are a few good walking shoes, shoes designed for running are usually better for walking. Not only do they have more research behind them, But with so many are more choices you're more likely to find one that fits and works better on your feet. As you read further, you'll see that the process of fitting a shoe involves trying several, and comparing them, while hopefully drawing upon the advice of shoe experts. I want you to control the process by narrowing down and then picking the one that works best.

Bring your most worn pair of shoes with you

A running store sales person can tell a lot about your stride by the pattern of wear on a well-used walking or street shoe. Primarily, shoe wear reveals the way your foot rolls. Once an experienced staff person determines this, he or she can tell how your foot functions, and recommend a shoe that best supports your foot in the walking motion.

How to get the best shoe—for you!

- **Demonstrate your stride**

  A knowledgeable shoe store staff person can usually notice how your foot functions ... by watching you walk. This is a skill gained through the experience of fitting thousands of feet, and from comparing notes with other staff members who are even more experienced (a daily practice in the better stores).

- **Feedback is important**

  Start by telling your staff person you are planning to walk, the surface you use, aches or pains, and any other issues (past foot damage, shape issues, etc.). As you work with the person in the store you need to give feedback as to how the shoe fits and feels. You want the shoe to protect your foot while usually allowing the foot to go through a natural walking motion for you. Tell the staff person if there are pressure points or pains—or a shoe just doesn't feel right.

- **Share information about injuries or foot problems**

  If you have had some structural damage (skiing accident, football injury) tell your shoe expert. If you've experienced some joint issues (knee, hip, ankle) or any condition possibly caused by the motion of your foot called "over pronation" (see sidebar below) you may need a shoe that protects your foot from this excess motion. Try several shoes in the "structure" category to see which seems to feel best—while helping to keep the pronation under control.

- **Not every foot needs fixing**

  Even if your foot rolls excessively one way or the other, you don't necessarily need to get an over-controlling shoe. The leg and foot make many adjustments and adaptations which keep many walkers injury free—even when they have extreme motion.

- **The best shoes aren't always the most expensive**

  The most expensive shoes are usually not the best shoes for most feet. You cannot assume that high price will buy you extra protection or more miles. At the price of some of the shoes, you might expect that they would take your walks for you. They won't.

No running store nearby?

1. Look at the wear pattern on your most worn pair of walking or street shoes. Use the guide below to help you choose about 3 pairs of shoes from one of the categories below:

    *   Floppy: Any wear on the inside of the forefoot—particularly on the edge of the inside forefoot
        If you have the wear pattern of a "floppy" or flexible foot, and have some foot or knee pain, look for a shoe that has "structure" or anti-pronation capabilities.
    *   Rigid: Wear on the outside of the forefoot of the shoe—no wear on the inside of forefoot
        A rigid foot pushes off within a narrow range of motion on the outside of the foot and usually responds well to a neutral shoe that has adequate cushion and flexibility for you, as you walk in them.
    *   Can't tell?
        If you don't have any foot or leg issues that require specific shoes, you can probably use a shoe that is fairly neutral (no motion control devices) and has an average amount of cushion and support.

2. Walk on a pavement surface to compare the shoes. If you have a floppy foot, make sure that you get the support you need. Again, if you have no injuries, aches or pains, don't get a shoe that has too much correction.

3. You want a shoe that feels natural on your foot—no pressure or aggravation—while allowing the foot to go through the range of motion that is comfortable for you when you walk naturally.

4. Ask questions! There are no stupid questions, so ask about anything that doesn't feel right or that you don't understand.

5. Take as much time as you need before deciding to buy a particular shoe.

6. If the store doesn't let you walk in the shoe, go to another store

Don't trust the size on the shoebox

Most running shoes are about 1-2 sizes larger than a street shoe which fits the same way. For example, I wear a size 10 street shoe but wear a size 12 running model. Be open to getting the best fit—regardless of what size you see on the label on the shoe or the box.

Leave some extra room for your toes

Your foot tends to swell during the day, so it's best to fit your shoes after noontime. Be sure to stand up in the shoe during the fitting process to measure how much extra room you have in the toe region of the shoe when standing. Pay attention to the longest of your feet, and leave at least half an inch.

Width issues

- Running shoes tend to be a bit wider than street shoes.
- Usually, the lacing can "snug up" the difference, if your foot is a bit narrower.
- The shoe shouldn't be laced too tight around your foot because the foot swells during a walk. On hot days, the average walker will move up one-half shoe size.

- In general, running shoes are designed to handle a certain amount of "looseness". But if you are getting blisters when wearing a loose shoe, snug the laces.
- Several shoe companies have some shoes in widths. I don't recommend going to width sizing unless you cannot get a good fit with conventional shoes.

Buying women's shoes

Women's shoes tend to be slightly narrower than those for men, and the heel is usually a bit smaller. The quality of the major running shoe brands is equal whether for men or women. But about 25% of women walkers have feet that can fit better into men's shoes. Usually the confusion comes in women who wear large sizes. The better running stores can help you sort through the choices.

If the shoe color doesn't match your outfit, it's not the end of the world

I receive several emails every year about injuries that were produced by wearing the wrong shoe. Some of these are "fashion injuries" in which the walker picked a shoe because the shoe color matched the outfit. Remember that there are no fashion police out there.

Breaking in a new shoe

- Wear the new shoe around the house, for a few minutes each day for a week. If you stay on carpet, and the shoe doesn't fit correctly, you can exchange it at the store. But if you have put some wear on the shoe (dirt, etc.) few stores will take it back.

- In most cases you will find that the shoe feels comfortable enough to walk immediately. It is best to continue walking around the house only, gradually allowing the foot to accommodate to the arch, the heel, the ankle pads, and to make other adjustments. If you walk too much in the shoe, too soon, blisters can result.

- If there are no rubbing issues on the foot when walking, you could walk in the new shoe for a gradually increasing amount, for 2-4 days.

- On the first walk, don't go farther than about half a mile in the shoe. Put on your old shoes and continue the walking distance for that day.

- On each successive walk, increase the distance covered in the new shoe for 3-4 outings. At this point, you will usually have the new shoe broken in.

When is the right time to buy new shoes?

1. When you have been using a shoe for 3-4 weeks successfully, go back to the store quickly and buy another pair of exactly the same model, make, size, etc. The reason for this: The shoe companies often make significant changes or discontinue shoe models (even successful ones) every 6-8 months.

2. Walk around the house in the new shoe for a few days.

3. After the shoe feels broken in, walk a half mile on one of your weekly walks in the new shoe, then put on the shoe that is already broken in.

4. On the "shoe break-in" day, gradually walk a little more in the new shoe. Continue to do this only one day a week.

5. Several weeks later you will notice that the new shoe offers more bounce than the old one.

6. When the old shoe doesn't offer the support you need, shift to the new pair.

7. Start breaking in a third pair.

GETTING "HOOKED" ON WALKING

If you choose to take charge, you would be surprised how much control you have over that part of life that revolves around exercise. The way you schedule your walks, your rewards, and your challenges will significantly influence your motivation and this will determine the number of walks you get in per week. But you also can control how good you will feel during each walk and how quickly you will recover.

In a walking program, there is no need to ever experience pain But this puts on you, the new walker, the responsibility of never making a big jump in the amount of exercise that you will do at one time. All of this will be explained later in this book, but you can have fun when you walk—every single day if you hold yourself back and don't spend all of the resources early.

My first bit of advice concerning motivation is to start keeping a training journal. Flip through the journal, look ahead, and write down the three days a week you will walk, each week for 2-3 weeks. Be sure to pick a time then the temperature is OK for you, and a segment of the day when you should have open time. Lock it in! The commitment to yourself to simply get out there 3 times a week will be reinforced significantly by writing it down. The final link in the motivational chain is to make sure that you walk on the designated days. If you wait until the spirit moves you to walk, you will probably have many empty spaces on your training journal. You must also be in charge of the little things that keep the schedule filled—such as spending a few minutes a week to plan your weekly sessions, and to reward yourself afterward.

- Regularity is important for the body and the mind. When you have 3 exercise-free days in a row between walks, you start to lose some of your ongoing conditioning and adaptations.

- Every other day is better than walking 2 or 3 days in a row—at the beginning of your training program. Having a day off between walks lets the leg muscles rebuild and rebound more quickly. You'll find yourself looking forward to the next one. Also, your mind and spirit are more likely to pull you out on your next walk, if you schedule it every second day.

Enjoying the first three weeks – a top priority

A high percentage of those who follow the schedule below for 3 weeks will continue for 6 months. So, write down your schedule or follow the successful one below for the next 21 days. Stick to it. After exercising now for about half a century I can tell you that the first 3 weeks are crucial for making exertion a positive habit in your life—one you really look forward to.

Rules for each walk day

1. Walk at a time of the day when the temperature is comfortable.

2. If the weather doesn't cooperate, have an indoor alternative: treadmill, indoor track, indoor space where walking is allowed, etc.

3. No huffing and puffing is allowed. Walk at a slow pace for 10-15 minutes, then ease into the speed of walking that is comfortable for you—on that day.

4. As much as possible, pick a pleasing venue to walk

5. Reward yourself afterward: a smoothie, another snack, new shoes, new outfit

Six month of walking, and you'll be hooked for life!

Most of those who continue for half a year develop a positive addiction to walking—and a very high percentage continue for life. In this book you will receive a schedule that lasts for 6 months. You can break this up any way you wish. Some walkers like to focus on one week at a time, others a month… while others 3-6 months. Do what is motivating for you. Right now, however, we will focus on the first week.

Once a week, a special walk…and each month, too

It helps most beginners to schedule a special walk each week—in a scenic area or with a motivating person or group. Each month, plan to walk in a local 5K or regional festive event. Don't think that these events are only for runners or seasoned competitors. Most of the events are experiencing larger growth in walkers than runners. Whether walking or running—participants enter because they enjoy the experience, and want to wear the race T-shirt.

Veteran walkers who've walked for 20 years or more tend to have the following things in common:

1. They enjoy most of the miles almost every day
2. They take extra days off from walking to recover from aches, pains, and burnout
3. They don't let themselves get stuck in a rut,but add variety, regularly.
4. They don't let 3 days go by without taking a walk— even a short one.

Walking with others is very motivating

Talk with family members or co-workers about joining you. Having someone to share the walk will motivate you to get going, and keep you going. Weekly (or more frequent) walks with parents, kids, spouse or co-workers will become special experiences that will enhance your relationship... and your life.

YOUR FIRST WEEK—GETTING STARTED AND KEEPING GOING

Schedule

Monday	Tuesday	Wednesday
5 min very slow	Off	5 min very slow
5-10 min regular walk		8-15 min reg
5-10 min warm down		5-10 min warm down

Thursday	Friday	Saturday	Sunday
Off	5 min v. slow	Off	5 min v. slow
	12-18 min reg		15-23 min reg
	5-10 min warm		5-10 min warm
	down		down

Venues: Home, work, kid's activity area...

The easier it is to get out the door, the more likely you will be to exercise. The most common venues are the following:

1. In your neighborhood, before the rest of the family has awakened
2. At noon, from your worksite
3. After work before other family members have arrived—or with friends or family members
4. After dinner—with other family members
5. When you are waiting for someone. Soccer moms or dads (etc.) walk around the practice field, for example.

Caffeine, anyone?

Many exercisers have a cup of coffee, tea, or diet drink about an hour before they walk to get the central nervous system ready to go. If your blood sugar level is low due to any reason (especially in the afternoon), eat about half of an energy bar or 100-200 calories of a sports drink—especially one that has about 20% protein—about 25-30 min before the start of the walk. If you have problems with caffeine, don't use it.

Your walking stride

Keep your feet low to the ground, lightly touching. Don't lift your knees. In general, make it easy on yourself. You want to get into a groove when walking so that you don't feel the muscles, feet, joints, because everything is working together within a range of motion for which you are designed. Slow and gentle walking produces few, if any, aches and pains. Long strides, however, will increase the chance of injury. For the first two months I recommend gentle walking.

The first walk

1. Put on a comfortable pair of running or walking shoes.
2. Put on light, comfortable clothes—see "clothing thermo-meter" in this book.
   Note: clothes don't have to be designed for exercise—just comfortable.
3. Walk for 5 minutes at a very slow pace to warm the muscles up gently.
4. If the legs are moving well and naturally, increase to a normal walk pace, for you.
5. Get into a smooth motion that feels very comfortable to you.
6. Do this for 5-10 minutes—no more.
7. Walk slowly for 5-10 minutes as a "warm-down."

First, the warm-up

By walking for 5 minutes, very slowly, you will gently move the tendons and ligaments through the necessary range of motion. At the same time, you'll send blood into the muscles, as you get the heart, lungs and circulation system ready for gentle exertion. Your nerve system can get into "synch" when you have at least 5 minutes of easy movement as a warm-up. If you need more minutes of slow walking, continue doing so.

What? No stretching?

That's right. I see no reason to stretch before a walk, unless you have some unusual problem that has been helped by stretching. The ilio-tibial band injury is one of these exceptions. I've found, after working with over 150,000 exercisers through the years that stretching causes many injuries, with no benefits for most.

No huffing and puffing allowed

Don't let the level of exertion get to the point that you must huff and puff. You want to be able to talk or sing, as you do your walking. This is called the "talk test."

Warm down

Just walk easily for 5-10 minutes. It is important that you keep moving the legs slowly after the walk. Don't ever go right into the shower after a vigorous walk, and don't stand around immediately after exertion either. This can be very stressful on your heart.

The day after

The next day, after your first walk, take the day off from exercise. After a few weeks you will have the option to take a short walk on these "easy days" but let's work on recovery at the beginning.

Your second walk

Two days after your first walk, it's your "workout day" again. As long as you have recovered quickly from the first day, repeat the same routine as the first time, but extend the length by 3-5 minutes. If you haven't fully recovered, walk very slowly the whole time—and keep your stride very short and gentle.

Alternate your workout days

Continue to do your walk about every other day, with a day off between (or an easy 10 minutes of walking). As long as the legs and body are recovering, you could continue increasing the middle segment by an additional 3-5 minutes until the total reaches 30 minutes—see the schedule that follows this chapter. The warm up and warm down periods can stay the same.

Regularity

....is extremely important during the first 8 weeks. On a very busy day, if it is your walk day, get in at least a 5 minute walk. Even this short a period will help to maintain most of the adaptations. Naturally it is better to do more than this, but 5 minutes is better than zero. If you wait 3 days between walks, you start to lose the adaptations, and your body complains a bit longer into each walk. Getting into a habit is the most helpful way to make it past 3 weeks.

It's OK to do no exercise on the day between walks

Focus on your every-other-day walks as "appointments," and make each one of them.

Reward yourself!

After you have finished your first week of three sessions, congratulate yourself with a special exercise outfit, meal, trip to a scenic walk area, etc. Remember that rewards can be very powerful.

Congratulations! You're on your way!

YOUR THREE-WEEK
SCHEDULE

*"The first three weeks are the most important
in your exercise life!"*

If you can set up your walking habit during the next three weeks—only 9 sessions—you have about an 80% chance of continuing walking for 6 months, according to my experience. The members of the "six month club" tend to continue as life-long exercisers. Here are some tips for your 21 day mission:

- Find a place in your schedule when you are very likely to have time to walk. For most people this means getting up 30 minutes early. Go to bed 30 minutes early. But even if you don't, you should be fine with 30 min less sleep. The overwhelming response from exercisers I've worked with, who've initially said they couldn't live without those 30 minutes (but gave it a try), is...they really had no problem. The vitality you gain from your walk will energize the rest of your day.

- Get your spouse, significant other, friends, co-workers, etc., to be your support team. Promise that if you get through the next 3 weeks having done the walks, that you will have a party for them, picnic, whatever. Pick supportive people who will email you, and will be supportive during and after the training, and the celebration.

- Have a friend or three who you can call, in case you have low motivation day. Just the voice on the phone can usually get you out the door. Of course it is always better to have a positive and enthusiastic person in this role.

- It is best to also have a back-up time to walk. The usual times for this are at noon or after work.

- While commuter traffic is high, get in your walk: some get to work very early, and others walk immediately after work.

- If necessary, you can break up your walk into several segments: morning, lunch hour, after dinner.

- At first it is best to walk only on the walk days noted on the schedule. After you get through the first 2 months, you may start adding an optional short walk on the "rest day" between.

Remember, no huffing and puffing—and maintain a short stride!

Week 2

Mission: You are continuing to increase distance. On Sunday, pick a scenic place for your walk.

Mon	Tue	Wed	Thurs	Fri	Sat	Sun
15-18 min	Off	17-19 min	Off	19-21min	off	21-23 min

Week 3

Mission: You're really making progress now—getting up near the half hour mark! On Saturday, ask some friends to go with you for the warm up and warm down—and have a picnic afterward. You've made it 3 weeks. Keep going, you have an easy week coming.

Mon	Tue	Wed	Thurs	Fri	Sat	Sun
Off	23-25min	off	25-27min	off	28-30 min	off

Week 4

Mission: Rest a bit. This is an easier week, to make sure the body catches up. You have earned this. It's time for your 3 week party. Pick the day and the place, and celebrate.

Mon	Tue	Wed	Thurs	Fri	Sat	Sun
20-22 min	off	20 min	off	25 min	off	22 min

You will do this! Just focus on each day, and make the little adjustments that you need to make.

While you are doing your walks, you can plan your 3 week success party. If you pick the right people, you may just have some converts and some companions who will join you in your mission and walk with you!

"You've made it through the toughest part of the program, you only need to maintain momentum, now."

YOUR NEXT
21 WEEKS

"Once you make your walks a permanent item on your weekly calendar, you're hooked—in a good way"

Now that you have invested so much of yourself in the progress and lifestyle changes, it's time to enjoy more of your walks, while focusing on the 6 month goal. Feel free to pick a different fun activity each week: different course, different person to walk with, etc.

It's time to pick your program!

Below you will find 3 programs, based upon how quickly you want to progress. At the end of the chapter you will find a continuing program for the rest of the year..

- The Gold program is for those who have followed the schedule to date and are feeling strong

- The Silver program is for those who want to increase more slowly and/or have had aches and pains

- The Fat-Burning program has more exercise time. All walks should be done very slowly.

Here's how the schedule works

1. Every week, I will suggest a slight increase in the amount of walking.

2. You can include the warm up and the warm down as part of your total—or you can separate it out as "extra credit" for fat-burning.

3. I've included a 10 minute walk, every other day—which is optional. After week 15, you can increase this to 15 minutes if you wish.

4. The important days are the longer days—you don't need to walk the short days for conditioning but this is helpful for fat-burning).

5. If the amount assigned is too much for you right now, then reduce it to a comfortable level. When you reach a level of exercise that feels "right" for you, maintain that level for as long as you wish before moving on.

6. At week #10, I set the long walk day as Saturday. If you prefer Sunday, walk for 10 minutes on Friday, take Saturday off, and do the long walk on Sunday.

7. You are the captain of your ship—make changes that work for you and your schedule.

Gold Program
for those who have followed the schedule to date and continue feeling strong

Mon	Tue	Wed	Thur	Fri	Sat	Sun
Week 5						
24-26 min	10 min	24-26 min	10 min	26-28 min	off	30 min
Week 6						
10 min	30 min	10 min	30 min	off	33 min	10 min
Week 7						
23 min	10 min	23 min	10 min	25 min	off	25 min
Week 8						
10 min	30 min	10 min	30 min	off	36 min	10 min
Week 9						
30 min	10 min	33 min	10 min	33 min	off	39 min
Week 10						
10 min	25 min	10 min	27 min	off	27 min	12 min
Week 11						
10 min	33 min	10 min	33 min	off	39 min	15 min
Week 12						
10 min	33 min	10 min	33 min	off	42 min	15 min
Week 13						
10 min	30 min	10 min	30-35 min	off	35 min	15 min
Week 14						
10 min	30 min	10 min	30-35 min	off	45 min	15 min
Week 15						
10 min	30 min	10 min	30-35 min	off	48 min	15 min
Week 16						
10 min	30 min	10 min	35-40 min	off	38 min	15 min
Week 17						
10 min	30 min	10 min	35-40 min	off	51 min	15 min

Week 18

| 10 min | 30 min | 10 min | 35-40 min | off | 54 min | 15 min |

Week 19

| 10 min | 30 min | 10 min | 35-40 min | off | 41 min | 15 min |

Week 20

| 10 min | 30 min | 10 min | 38-45 min | off | 57 min | 15 min |

Week 21

| 10 min | 30 min | 10 min | 38-45 min | off | 60 min | 15 min |

Week 22

| 10 min | 30 min | 10 min | 38-45 min | off | 45 min | 15 min |

Week 23

| 10 min | 30 min | 10 min | 38-45 min | off | 60 min | 15 min |

Week 24

| 10 min | 30 min | 10 min | 38-45 min | off | 60 min | 15 min |

Week 25

| 10 min | 30 min | 10 min | 38-45 min | off | 45 min | 15 min |

Week 26

| 10 min | 30 min | 10 min | 38-45 min | off | 60 min | 15 min |

*Note:
Continue by alternating week # 25 and week # 26 or, choose one of the training programs in this book—for the 5K, 10K or Half Marathon.

Silver Program
for those who want to go a bit slower, or have had some aches and pains

Mon	Tue	Wed	Thur	Fri	Sat	Sun
			Week 5			
20 min	off	20 min	10 min	26-28 min	off	30 min
			Week 6			
10 min	22 min	10 min	22 min	off	30 min	10 min
			Week 7			
22 min	off	22 min	10 min	22 min	off	22 min
			Week 8			
10 min	24 min	10 min	24 min	off	33 min	10 min
			Week 9			
22 min	off	22 min	10 min	22 min	off	36 min
			Week 10			
10 min	20 min	off	20 min	off	25 min	10 min
			Week 11			
10 min	24 min	off	33 min	off	36 min	10 min
			Week 12			
10 min	24 min	10 min	33 min	off	39 min	10 min
			Week 13			
10 min	24 min	10 min	30 min	off	30 min	10 min
			Week 14			
10 min	26 min	10 min	30-33 min	off	41 min	15 min
			Week 15			
10 min	26 min	10 min	30-33 min	off	43 min	15 min
			Week 16			
10 min	26 min	10 min	35 min	off	39 min	15 min
			Week 17			
10 min	28 min	10 min	35min	off	45 min	15 min

			Week 18			
10 min	28 min	10 min	35min	off	47 min	15 min
			Week 19			
10 min	28 min	10 min	35min	off	41 min	15 min
			Week 20			
10 min	30 min	10 min	38min	off	49 min	15 min
			Week 21			
10 min	30 min	10 min	38min	off	51 min	15 min
			Week 22			
10 min	30 min	10 min	38-45 min	off	43 min	15 min
			Week 23			
10 min	30 min	10 min	38min	off	53 min	15 min
			Week 24			
10 min	30 min	10 min	38min	off	55 min	15 min
			Week 25			
10 min	30 min	10 min	38min	off	45 min	15 min
			Week 26			
10 min	30 min	10 min	38min	off	58 min	15 min

*Note:
Continue by alternating week # 25 and week # 26 or, choose one of the training programs in this book—for the 5K, 10K or Half Marathon.

Fat Burning Program

The time spent walking increases significantly, so keep the pace very slow. The idea is to keep from huffing and puffing as you increase the distance covered. You can do two sessions a day with the exception of the Saturday session. This is the long one and should be done at one time. See the fat burning chapter for more details on how more miles of easy exercise promotes fat burning.

Mon	Tue	Wed	Thur	Fri	Sat	Sun
			Week 5			
24-26 min	10 min	26 min	10 min	28 min	off	30 min
			Week 6			
10 min	33 min	10 min	33 min	off	35 min	10 min
			Week 7			
23 min	10 min	29 min	10 min	25 min	off	30 min
			Week 8			
12 min	33 min	12 min	33 min	off	38 min	12 min
			Week 9			
33 min	12 min	33 min	12 min	33 min	off	39 min
			Week 10			
15 min	28 min	15 min	30 min	off	30 min	15 min
			Week 11			
15 min	36 min	15 min	36 min	off	42 min	15 min
			Week 12			
15 min	39 min	15 min	39 min	off	45 min	15 min
			Week 13			
18 min	30 min	18 min	35 min	off	38 min	18 min
			Week 14			
18 min	42 min	18 min	42 min	off	48 min	18 min
			Week 15			
18 min	45 min	18 min	45 min	off	52 min	18 min

Week 16						
20 min	35 min	18 min	35 min	off	45 min	20 min
Week 17						
20 min	48 min	18 min	48min	off	55 min	20 min
Week 18						
20 min	51 min	18 min	51min	off	58 min	20 min
Week 19						
20 min	40 min	18 min	40 min	off	45 min	20 min
Week 20						
20 min	54 min	20 min	54 min	off	60 min	20 min
Week 21						
20 min	58 min	20 min	58 min	off	65 min	20 min
Week 22						
20 min	45 min	20 min	45 min	off	45 min	20 min
Week 23						
20 min	60 min	20 min	60 min	off	70 min	20 min
Week 24						
20 min	60 min	20 min	60 min	off	73 min	20 min
Week 25						
20 min	45 min	20 min	45 min	off	45 min	20 min
Week 26						
20 min	60 min	20 min	60 min	off	75 min	20 min

*Note:
Continue by alternating week # 25 and week # 26 or, choose one of the training programs in this book—for the 5K, 10K or Half Marathon.

TRAINING PROGRAMS 5K * 10K * HALF MARATHON * MARATHON

Thousands of walkers every year get hooked on exercise because they enter a race—with no illusions of winning. It may be a challenge from a co-worker or relative, a mid-life crisis when struggling to climb a short stairway, or the desire to collect pledges for a charity by training for a marathon. The most common ingredients for success are, 1) writing the event date on a calendar, and 2) telling others about the goal. For the record, there are worse addictions.

Endurance

The primary ingredient in a training program is the long walk. If you want to prepare adequately for a 5K you need to gradually increase the long one up to 4 miles....and up to 26 miles for a marathon. By using "shuffle" breaks, and walking gently, the body responds to each small increase in distance by adapting in many physiological ways.

Maintenance

To maintain the adaptations and conditioning of the long one, you only need to walk for 30 minutes, two other times a week. It is OK to walk more if the body is recovering well from the weekend walks. Occasionally, one may only walk for 15 minutes on these short days—but regularity is important.

Satisfaction

Few activities in life bring more internal satisfaction than the continual pushing of the barriers of endurance toward a goal. Every week I hear from those who used the programs below to turn their fitness life around. They could barely walk around the block at the beginning of their training. Six months later, after finishing a half marathon or marathon they feel empowered to do more in significant areas of their lives.

Rules

1. Count back from the goal date, and write the distances below on a calendar or training journal (see the journal chapter in this book). First write the long ones—then the maintenance walks.
2. Remember that the long one must be done slowly with shuffle breaks—from the beginning.
3. Use a short stride, feet low to the ground, light touch of the foot. Your goal is to feel no effort and no pain as you walk. Never keep walking when you experience pain. Stop and find out what caused it.
4. Don't do any exercise the day before your long one—except incidental walking to work, shop, etc.
5. Beginners should finish one of the three schedules in the previous chapter before starting one of the following schedules. Others should build their walks to the duration of those in the first week of the chosen schedule.
6. On the days between walks (the "off" days), it is OK to do alternative exercise that doesn't fatigue the walking muscles. Stair machines or spinning classes are out, but short walks, gentle cycling, swimming, etc. are fine.
7. It is best for beginners who want to train for a longer event to go through the 5K training program first, then start the other program, etc.
8. Veteran walkers, who have been walking, every other day, for more than a year, and walk 3 miles or more regularly, can come into any program, at the length of the last long one—within the last 2 weeks. In other words, if you had a 7 mile walk two weeks ago, find the long one on the schedule that is that distance. This would determine the week where you could start.

9. It is important to do the maintenance walks on Tuesday and Thursday. If you are "time challenged" you can walk as little as 15 minutes on a few of these days—but please get in at least 30 minutes on the other days as assigned on the schedule.

10. If you are already doing more than the amount on the maintenance days (30 minutes), you can continue to do the increased amount as long as you are recovering between weekend walks.

The schedules

5K

Mon	Tue	Wed	Thu	Fri	Sat	Sun
1. off	30 min walk	off	30 min walk	easy walk	off	2.5 miles
2. off	30 min walk	off	30 min walk	easy walk	off	2.75 miles
3. off	30 min walk	off	30 min walk	easy walk	off	3.0 miles
4. off	30 min walk	off	30 min walk	easy walk	off	3.25 miles
5. off	30 min walk	off	30 min walk	easy walk	off	3.5 miles
6. off	30 min walk	off	30 min walk	easy walk	off	3.75 miles
7. off	30 min walk	off	30 min walk	easy walk	off	4.0 miles
8. off	30 min walk	off	30 min walk	easy walk	off	5K event
9. off	30 min walk	off	30 min walk	easy walk	off	4.0 miles
10. off	30 min walk	off	30 min walk	easy walk	off	3.0 miles or 5K

10K

(assumes completion of a 5K program or a 4 mile walk within 2 weeks of starting this program)

Mon	Tue	Wed	Thu	Fri	Sat	Sun
1. off	30 min walk	off	30 min walk	easy walk	off	4.5 miles
2. off	30 min walk	off	30 min walk	easy walk	off	3.0 miles or 5K
3. off	30 min walk	off	30 min walk	easy walk	off	5.0 miles

	Mon	Tue	Wed	Thu	Fri	Sat	Sun
4.	off	30 min walk	off	30 min walk	easy walk	off	3.0 miles
5.	off	30 min walk	off	30 min walk	easy walk	off	5.5 miles
6.	off	30 min walk	off	30 min walk	easy walk	off	3.0 miles or 5K
7.	off	30 min walk	off	30 min walk	easy walk	off	6.0 miles
8.	off	30 min walk	off	30 min walk	easy walk	off	3.0 miles or 5K
9.	off	30 min walk	off	30 min walk	easy walk	off	6.5 miles
10.	off	30 min walk	off	30 min walk	easy walk	off	3.0 miles
11.	off	30 min walk	off	30 min walk	easy walk	off	7.0 miles
12.	off	30 min walk	off	30 min walk	easy walk	off	3.0 miles
13.	off	30 min walk	off	30 min walk	easy walk	off	10K event
14.	off	30 min walk	off	30 min walk	easy walk	off	3.0 miles

Half Marathon

(Assumes either completion of 10K program or a long walk of 7 miles within 2 weeks of starting this program)

	Mon	Tue	Wed	Thu	Fri	Sat	Sun
1.	off	30 min walk	off	30 min walk	easy walk	off	8 miles
2.	off	30 min walk	off	30 min walk	easy walk	off	4 miles
3.	off	30 min walk	off	30 min walk	easy walk	off	9 miles
4.	off	30 min walk	off	30 min walk	easy walk	off	4 miles
5.	off	30 min walk	off	30 min walk	easy walk	off	10 miles
6.	off	30 min walk	off	30 min walk	easy walk	off	5 miles
7.	off	30 min walk	off	30 min walk	easy walk	off	11 miles
8.	off	30 min walk	off	30 min walk	easy walk	off	5 miles
9.	off	30 min walk	off	30 min walk	easy walk	off	12 miles
10.	off	30 min walk	off	30 min walk	easy walk	off	5 miles
11.	off	30 min walk	off	30 min walk	easy walk	off	13 miles
12.	off	30 min walk	off	30 min walk	easy walk	off	5 miles
13.	off	30 min walk	off	30 min walk	easy walk	off	14 miles
14.	off	30 min walk	off	30 min walk	easy walk	off	5 miles
15.	off	30 min walk	off	30 min walk	easy walk	off	Half Marathon
16.	off	30 min walk	off	30 min walk	easy walk	off	5 miles

Marathon

(assumes either completion of a half marathon program or a long one of 14 miles within 2 weeks of starting this program)

	Mon	Tue	Wed	Thu	Fri	Sat	Sun
1.	off	30 min walk	off	30 min walk	easy walk	off	15 miles
2.	off	30 min walk	off	30 min walk	easy walk	off	5 miles
3.	off	30 min walk	off	30 min walk	easy walk	off	16.5 miles
4.	off	30 min walk	off	30 min walk	easy walk	off	5 miles
5.	off	30 min walk	off	30 min walk	easy walk	off	18 miles
6.	off	30 min walk	off	30 min walk	easy walk	off	6 miles
7.	off	30 min walk	off	30 min walk	easy walk	off	20 miles
8.	off	30 min walk	off	30 min walk	easy walk	off	7 miles
9.	off	30 min walk	off	30 min walk	easy walk	off	22 miles
10.	off	30 min walk	off	30 min walk	easy walk	off	7 miles
11.	off	30 min walk	off	30 min walk	easy walk	off	7 miles
12.	off	30 min walk	off	30 min walk	easy walk	off	24 miles
13.	off	30 min walk	off	30 min walk	easy walk	off	7 miles
14.	off	30 min walk	off	30 min walk	easy walk	off	7 miles
15.	off	30 min walk	off	30 min walk	easy walk	off	26 miles
16.	off	30 min walk	off	30 min walk	easy walk	off	7 miles
17.	off	30 min walk	off	30 min walk	easy walk	off	7 miles
20.	off	30 min walk	off	30 min walk	easy walk	off	Marathon
21.	off	30 min walk	off	30 min walk	easy walk	off	4-6 miles
22.	off	30 min walk	off	30 min walk	easy walk	off	6-8 miles
23.	off	30 min walk	off	30 min walk	easy walk	off	6-20 miles

"SHUFFLING" TO CONTROL FATIGUE, SORENESS, ACHES

*"Shuffling is barely moving your feet and legs,
to let the walking muscles recover"*

In the "Walking Form" chapter you will find suggestions to reduce aches and pains and walk more efficiently. Most of the time you're doing it right if you feel comfortable, aren't huffing and puffing, and don't have any aches or pains after your first 10 minutes of walking. You are the captain of your walking ship and it is you who determines how far, how fast, how much you will walk, etc.

What is a "shuffle"?

With your feet next to the ground, use a short stride with minimal movement. You're still moving forward, but not having to spend much energy doing so. When you insert 30-60 seconds of shuffling into a regular walk, every 1-5 minutes, your walking muscles relax and rest. This lowers the chance of aches and pains due to the constant use of the muscles, tendons, etc.

Shuffle before you get tired

Most of us, even when untrained, can walk for several miles before fatigue sets in, because walking is an activity that we are bio-engineered to do for hours. Many beginners get discouraged, however, because during the first session or two they don't feel that they are going as far as they should—and add a mile or two. During the extra mileage they often feel strong, and hardly tired. In a day or two they know otherwise as overused muscles complain.

The continuous use of the walking muscles and tendons—even when the walking pace feels completely comfortable—piles up the stress in our "weak links" producing aches, and pains much more quickly. If you shuffle before your walking muscles start to get tired, you recover instantly—increasing your capacity for exercise while reducing the chance of a next-day soreness attack.

A strategy that gives you control

You can't wait until you're tired—you must insert the shuffles from the beginning. In setting up a conservative strategy of walk/shuffle, you gain control over fatigue, soreness, and aches. Using this fatigue-reduction tool early gives you muscle strength and mental confidence to the end. Even when you don't need the extra muscle strength and resiliency bestowed by the method, you will feel better during and after your walk, and will finish knowing that you could have gone further, while recovering faster.

Shuffle breaks allow you a chance to enjoy every walk. By taking them early and often you can feel strong, even after a walk that is very long for you. Beginners will alternate frequently between segments of regular walking with shuffle segments. There is no need to reach the end of a walk feeling exhausted if you insert enough shuffle breaks on that day.

Shuffle Breaks....

- Give you control over your fatigue build-up
- Bestow confidence because you have a strategy
- Erase fatigue with each shuffle
- Push back your fatigue wall
- Allow for endorphins to collect during each shuffle break—you feel good!
- Break up the distance into manageable units. ("one more minute and I can shuffle")
- Speed recovery
- Reduce the chance of aches, pains and injury

- Allow you to feel good afterward—carrying on the rest of your day without debilitating fatigue
- Give you all of the endurance of the distance of each session—without the pain

Older and heavier runners benefit even more from shuffling Taking more frequent shuffles allow older and heavier runners to recover much faster—and feel as strong as lighter or younger runners at the same distance.

A short and very gentle shuffle

When in doubt, reduce the effort of the shuffle down to almost nothing. Keep the feet low to the ground, with baby steps, barely moving the legs.

No need to ever eliminate the shuffle breaks

Some beginners assume that they must work toward the day when they don't have to take any shuffle breaks at all. This is up to the individual, but is not recommended. Remember that you decide what ratio of walk-shuffle to use. I suggest that you adjust the ratio to how you feel on a given day.

Even the most experienced walker has a few "weak links" that are irritated from continuous use. Shuffling can manage these—or eliminate them.

How to keep track of the shuffle breaks

There are several watches which can be set to beep when it's time to shuffle, and then beep again when it's time to walk. Check my website (www.jeffgalloway.com) or a good running store for advice in this area.

How to use shuffle breaks

1. Beginners could walk for 2 minutes and shuffle for 30 seconds. If you feel good during and after the walk, continue with this ratio. If not, adjust the ratio until you feel good.

2. Shuffle breaks allow the body to warm up more easily. If your legs feel tight or you have some soreness, walk for a minute and shuffle for 20-30 seconds—for the first 10 minutes. As the legs loosen up, reduce the shuffles as necessary.

3. On walks longer than about 45 minutes, even experienced walkers find that a 30 second shuffle, after 5 min of walking, helps recovery, and reduces aches and pains.

4. On any given day, when you need more shuffling, do so. Don't ever be afraid to drop back to make the walk more fun, and less tiring.

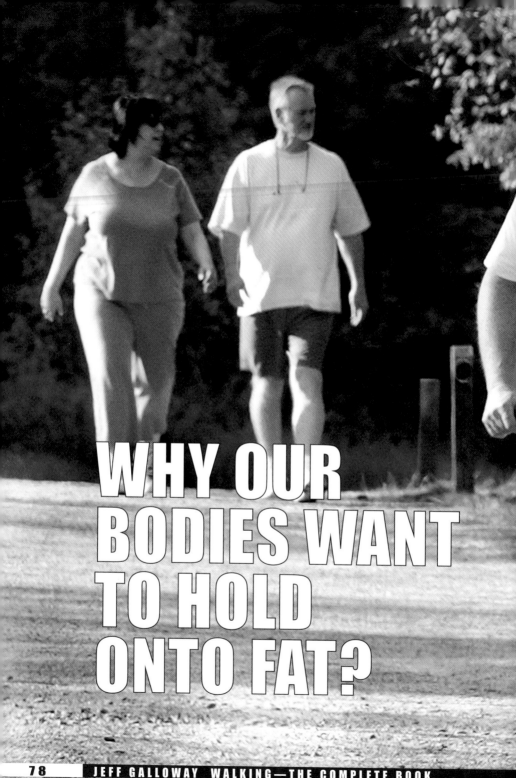

WHY OUR BODIES WANT TO HOLD ONTO FAT?

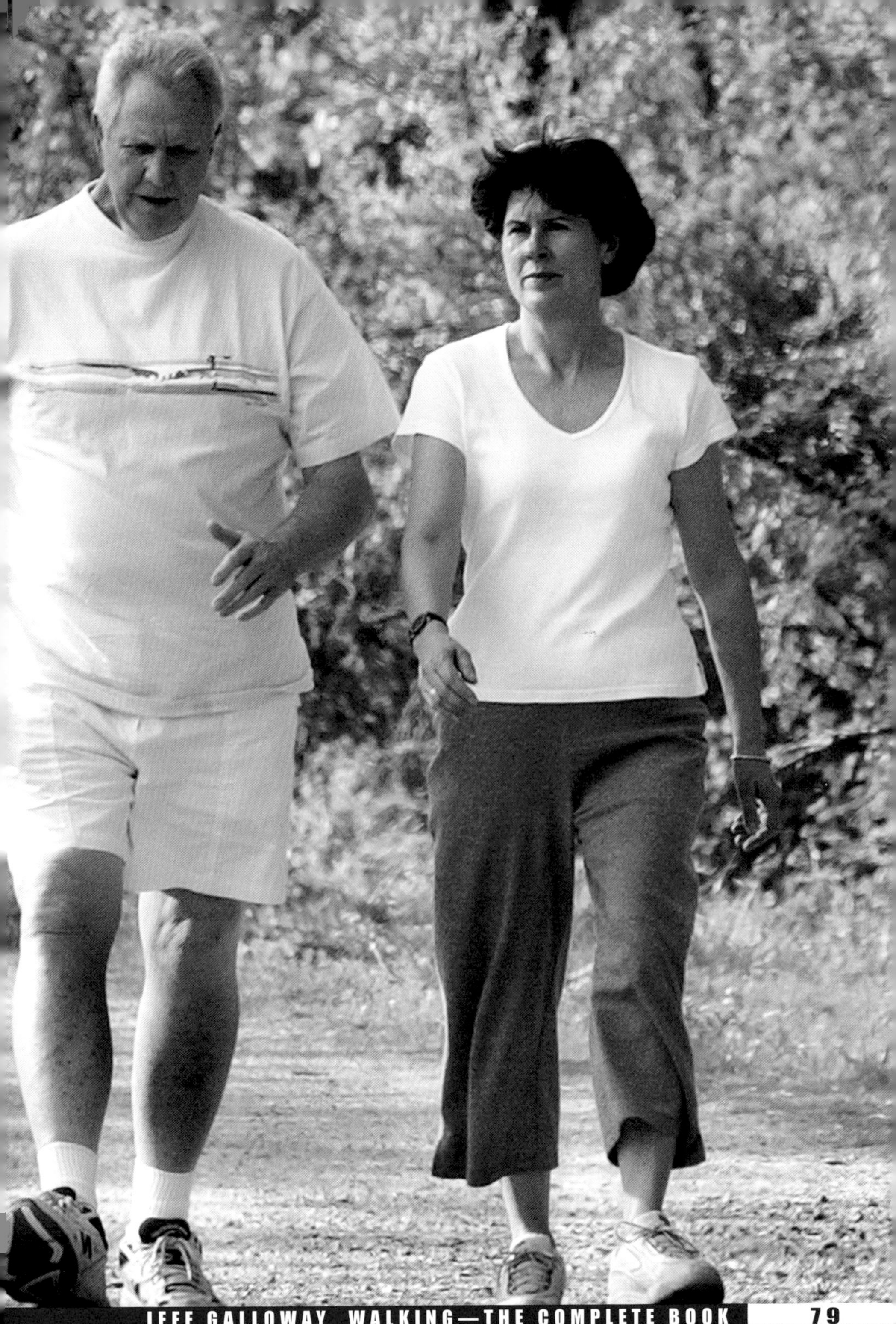

Fat is our biological insurance policy against disaster. It is the fuel your body can use in case of starvation, sickness, injury to the digestive system, etc. You'll read a bit later about how the "set point" inside you programs your body to hold onto fat too well. I've spent years looking into this topic, and talking to experts in the field. This chapter will explain my beliefs about the process so that you can gain control over your fat burning program.

Many people start walking to burn fat. Indeed, walking and running are probably the most effective and convenient exercise modes for burning fat and keeping it off. The fact is that endurance exercise makes the body into a fat-burning furnace. When the body is conditioned for fat burning, it prefers this fuel because of the small amount of waste product produced.

But it's not enough to burn the fat. For long term health and body management, you need to keep it off. Successful fat burners do 4 things:

1. Understand the process by reading this chapter and other sources.
2. Truly believe they can lower the body fat percentage.
3. Set up a behavioral plan of eating and exercising that accounts for the calorie flow.
4. Don't get obsessed with every calorie burned or eaten. They balance fat-burning with other activities in their lives and have a "reward food" every once in a while.

How does fat accumulate?

When you eat some fat during a snack or a meal, you might as well put it into a syringe and inject it into your stomach or thigh. A gram of fat eaten is a gram of fat processed and put into the fat storage areas on your body. In addition, when you eat more calories than you need during a day from protein (fish, chicken, beef, tofu) and carbohydrate (breads, fruits, vegetables, sugar), the excess is converted into fat and stored.

Fat for survival

After more than a million years of evolution your body is programmed to hold onto the fat you have stored because of a simple principle: the survival of the species. Before humans understood disease and prevention, they were susceptible to sweeping infections. Even mild diseases and flu wiped out a significant percentage of the population each year, in primitive times. Those who had adequate fat stores were more likely to survive periods of starvation and sickness, passing on the fat accumulation adaptation to their children.

The powerful set point holds onto our fat

The set point is a biologically engineered survival mechanism. While it does seem possible to adjust it, you are going into battle against biological mechanisms that have been in place for over a million years. By understanding it, however, you're in a better position to be in control of the process, and avoid getting obsessed.

Fat level is set in early 20s

Many experts agree that by about the age of 25 we have accumulated a level of fat that the body intuitively marks as it's lowest level. The set point is programmed to increase a little each year. Let's say that John had 10% body fat at age 25, and his set point increased by a tenth of a percent per year. The amount of increase is so small when we are young, that we usually don't realize we're adding it—until about 10 years later, when it's time to go to a class reunion or something.

We humans are supposed to carry around fat. But your set point does too good a job, continuing to add to the percentage, each year, every year. And the amount of increase seems to be significantly greater as we get older. Even when you've had a year when stress or illness prevented the usual increase, the set point makes it up by increasing appetite during the following year or two. Go ahead, shout "Unfair!" as loud as you wish. Your set point doesn't argue, it just sets you up for another deposit. Exercise can lower the set point...so hold onto your hope.

Men and women deposit fat differently

While men tend to deposit fat on the surface of the skin, women (particularly in their 20s and 30s) fill up internal storage areas first. Most young women will acknowledge that their weight is rising slightly, year by year, but aren't concerned because there is no noticeable fat increase on the surface. Some judge this by the "pinch test".

Then, during one year, the internal storage areas fill up, and the extra fat starts accumulating on the stomach, thighs and other areas. A common woman's complaint in the 30s or early 40s is the following: "My body has betrayed me." In fact, fat has been deposited at a fairly consistent rate but hidden from view for many years.

Men find it easier to burn fat than women

When men start running regularly, many lose fat and weight for several months. Probably related to biological issues, and primitive protections for mothers, women have a harder time losing fat. The reality is that you are ahead of the others in our society if you are even maintaining the same weight. Because of the set point, one would expect an average 45-year-old person in the US to gain 3-4 pounds a year. So the amount of body fat may be lowering even if you are holding at the same weight year to year—because of the increased blood volume, energy and fluid storage adaptations due to exercise.

Diets don't work because of the "starvation reflex"

We are certainly capable lowering food intake for days, weeks and months which can reduce fat levels and weight. This is a form of starvation, but the set point has a long-term memory. So we lose that 10 pounds during the 2 months before the class reunion. Then, when you stop the diet, you will experience a starvation reflex: a slight increase in appetite and hunger, over weeks and months until the fat accumulated on your body is higher than it was before the diet. It's a fact that almost all of those who lose fat on a diet put more pounds back on the body within months of going off the diet.

Waiting too long to eat triggers the starvation reflex

When you wait more than 3 hours without eating something, your set point organism senses that you may be going into a period of starvation. The longer you wait to eat, the more you will feel these three effects of the starvation reflex:

1. A reduction in your metabolism rate. Imagine an internal voice saying something like "if this person is going to start depriving me of food I had better tune down the metabolism rate to conserve resources." A slower metabolism makes you feel more lethargic, drowsy, and unmotivated to exercise or move around. In fact, you tend to stay in your chair or on the couch, minimizing motion and calorie burning—maintaining the fat on your body.

2. An increase in the fat-depositing enzymes. The longer you wait to eat something, the more enzymes you will have, and the more fat will be actually deposited from your next meal.

3. Your appetite increases. The longer you wait to eat, the more likely it is that, for the next few meals, you will have an insatiable appetite. In this state, you'll eat a normal meal but you're still hungry.

Suddenly depriving yourself of decadent foods

I used to like a particular type of ice cream so much that I ate a quart or more of it several nights a week. It was the reward I gave myself for reaching my exercise goals for that day. Then, on a fateful New Year's day, my wife Barb and I decided to eliminate the chocolate chip mint ice cream from our diet—after more than 10 years of enjoyment. We were successful for 2 years. A leftover box after a birthday party got us re-started on the habit, and we even increased our intake over what it had been before—due to having deprived ourselves.

You can "starve" yourself of a food that you dearly love for an extended period of time. But at some time in the future, when the food is around and no one else is.....you will over-consume that food. My correction for this problem was the following:

1. I made a contract with myself: I could have a little of it whenever I wanted—while promising to be "reasonable."
2. Setting a goal of enjoying one bowl a week, 5 years from now
3. Four years from now, enjoying a bowl every 4 days
4. Three years from now, a bowl every 3 days
5. Learning to enjoy healthy sweet things, like fruit salads, energy bars, etc.

It worked! I hardly ever eat any ice cream...but sometimes enjoy a bowl if I want. This is purely for medicinal reasons, you understand.

The low-carbohydrate scam

There is no doubt that low carb diets can help you lose weight....water weight. Such a loss is superficial and easily gained back. Here's how it works:

To perform physical exertion, you need a quick energy source called glycogen, which comes from eating carbohydrates, and must be replenished every day. The storage areas for glycogen are limited, and glycogen is also the primary source for vital organs like the brain. A good quantity of water is stored near the glycogen storage areas, because it is needed when glycogen is processed.

By starving themselves of carbohydrates, low carb dieters experience a severe reduction in glycogen. But if the glycogen isn't there, water is not stored either. The elimination of these two substances can produce a significant weight loss within days—continuing for a few weeks.

Fat is not being burned off. In fact, fat is encouraged in many of the low carb diets. As low carb dieters eat more fat, they often increase the fat on the body—while the water/glycogen loss will show a weight loss, due to the superficial loss of water. When they replace the water and glycogen later, the weight goes back on. Soon the overall body weight is greater than before because of the extra fat from the low carb diet.

Because the glycogen energy source is low or depleted, low carbers will not have the energy for endurance exercise. This is why you will hear folks on this diet complain of low energy, lack of desire to exercise, inability to finish a workout, and sometimes mental lack of focus (low glycogen means less fuel for the brain).

Even if you "tough it out" or cheat on the diet a little, your capacity to do even moderately strenuous exertions will be greatly reduced. With your energy stores near empty, exercising becomes a real struggle, and no fun.

Low carb diets don't tell you this...

- You don't burn fat—many gain fat
- The weight loss is usually water loss, with glycogen loss
- Almost everyone on this diet resumes regular eating, within a few weeks or months
- Almost all low carb dieters gain back more weight than they lost
- You lose the energy and motivation to exercise
- You lose exercise capacity that can help to keep the weight off when you resume normal eating
- Your metabolism rate goes down—making it harder to keep the weight off

This is a type of starvation diet. I've heard from countless low carb victims who admit that while they were on the diet, their psychological deprivation of carbs produced a significant rebound effect when they began eating them again. The cravings for bread, pastries, french fries, soft drinks, and other pound-adding foods, increased for months after they went off the diet. The weight goes back on, and on, and on.

Like so many diets, the low-carb diet reduces the metabolism rate. This reduces the number of calories you burn per day just living. When you return to eating a regular diet you will not have a "metabolism furnace" to burn up the increased calories.

Endurance exercise can lower the set point

Your body has a wonderful ability to adapt to the regular activities that you do. It also tries to avoid stress. In the next chapter we will talk about how to condition your muscles to be fat burning furnaces. Once you get them into shape to do this, you can move into a fat burning lifestyle. Lowering the set point is more complex, but possible—when you are regularly putting certain types of gentle but regular stress on your system year after year.

Endurance Exercise:

* a positive stress on the body
* which can stimulate adaptations in two areas:
  * body temperature increase
  * pounding or bouncing.

Walking regularly, long enough to produce these stresses, will trigger a search for ways of reducing the stress.

* **Increases core body temperature**
  Almost everyone who walks for more than 15 minutes gets warm or hot. The work required to lift your body over the ground raises your core body temperature. If you sustain this increase it puts a heat stress on the system. Since body fat acts like a blanket in maintaining body temperature, the body's intuitive, long- term solution is to reduce the size of the fat blanket around you, which then reduces the heat build-up.

The more regular you are with walks that build up to more than 45 minutes, the more likely it is that your set point will be reduced to avoid this repeated stress. It also helps even more to have one walk every week that goes beyond 90 minutes.

- **Bouncing and pounding**
  The more weight you carry, the more your internal monitoring mechanisms sense the pounding. If you walk as often as every other day, your body senses this regular stress and searches for ways of reducing it. It will tend to recognize that the reduction of the extra fat baggage will reduce the bouncing stress. As above, the 45 min/90 min time periods seem to be significant.

Cross training for fat burning

To maintain a regular dose of set-point lowering stress, while minimizing orthopedic stress, cross training helps. The best activities are those that raise core body temperature, use a lot of muscle cells, and can be continued comfortably for more than 45 minutes. Cross training is done on days when you don't walk. Swimming is not a good fat-burning exercise. The water absorbs temperature build-up, and therefore core body temperature doesn't rise significantly.

Good Fat Burning Exercises
• Nordic track
• Hiking
• Elliptical
• Rowing
• Exercise cycle

WHY SOME PEOPLE BURN A LOT MORE FAT...

Even if you don't lose a pound, if you walk regularly you'll receive a series of health benefits. Studies at the Cooper Clinic, founded by Dr. Kenneth Cooper in Dallas TX and other organizations, have shown that even obese people lower their risk factors for heart disease when they exercise regularly.

Slow, aerobic walking is one of the very best ways to burn fat. But most walkers, during their first year, usually hold their own, showing no weight loss. This is actually a victory over the set point. First, you are avoiding the average set point-inspired-increase of 3-4 pounds a year. But walkers are actually burning fat by maintaining weight. How can this be? Read on.

As you increase the distance of regular walks, your body stores more glycogen and water all over the body, to process energy, and cool you off. Your blood volume also increases. All of these internal changes help you exercise better, but they cause a weight gain (not a fat gain). If your weight is the same, a year after starting regular exercise, you have burned off several pounds of fat. Don't let the scales drive you crazy.

Long term fat burn off usually requires some discipline and focus. If you will take responsibility for managing your eating and doing the amount of walking needed, you will succeed. One secret to fat burning success is being more active all day long. Once you learn to walk instead of sit, you will be amazed at how many steps you will take per day:

Steps = Calories Burned

Aerobic walking burns fat

When you are walking within your physical capacity (no huffing and puffing), your muscles are being supplied with enough oxygen to do the work. They are aerobic. If you walk too hard or too long you overwhelm the capacity of the muscles, the blood system cannot deliver enough oxygen to the muscles and you shift into anaerobic exercise and burn the stored sugar in your muscles instead of fat.

Oxygen is needed to burn fat. Therefore walking at an easy pace will keep you in the aerobic, or "fat burning" zone. When you walk too fast, your muscles can't get enough oxygen and you will huff and puff. This is the sign that you are building up an oxygen debt.

Without oxygen, the muscles turn to stored glycogen, which produces a high amount of waste product.

Fat burning training program
- One long walk a week of 60 min + (later 90min +)
- Two walks of 45 min +
- 2-3 alternative exercise sessions of 45 min +
- Taking an additional 6000 (or more) steps a day in your daily activities

Sugar-burning during the first 15 min of exercise

Glycogen is the quick access fuel your body uses during the first quarter-hour of exercise. Those who don't exercise longer than 15 minutes will not get into fat burning, and won't train their muscles to burn this fuel very well. But if you have been depriving yourself of carbohydrates, as when on a low-carb diet, you'll have trouble with energy and motivation.

Glycogen produces a high amount of waste product—mostly lactic acid. If you move slowly, there is no significant build-up. Even when the pace feels slow, if you are huffing and puffing within the first 10 minutes, you have been going too fast. When in doubt, extend your walking at the beginning and go slower.

From 15 minutes to 45 minutes you will transition into fat burning

If you are exercising within your capabilities your body starts to break down body fat, and use it as fuel. Fat is actually a more efficient fuel, producing less waste product. This transition continues for the next 30 minutes or so. By the time you've been exercising within your capabilities for 45-50 minutes, you will be burning mostly fat—if the muscles are trained to do this. With easy walking and shuffling, almost anyone can work up to three sessions of 45 minutes each.

Three sessions a week, in the fat burn zone

Even the most un-trained muscles that have only burned glycogen for 50 years can be trained to burn fat under two conditions:

- Get into the fat-burning zone 3 times a week (45 + min a week)
- Do this regularly: 3 times a week. (best to have no more than two days between sessions)

One session a week beyond 90 minutes

The endurance session is designed to keep you in the fat burn zone for an extended period. For best results, this should be done every week, and should increase gradually to around 90 minutes. If you don't have time for a 90 minute session, shoot for 60 minutes at first, and extend it when you can.

"By walking for 90 minutes each week, the leg muscles become fat burners. Over time, this means that you will burn more fat when you are sitting around all day at your desk and even burn it when you are sleeping at night."

"Shuffle" breaks allow you to go farther without getting tired

The slowdown of shuffling reduces exertion and helps to keep you in the fat burn zone while allowing for a quick recovery of the muscles. For fat-burning purposes, it is best to shuffle earlier, and shuffle more often. The number of calories you burn is based upon the number of miles covered. Shuffle breaks allow you to cover more distance each day, without tiring yourself. By lowering the exertion level, you will stay in the fat burning zone longer—usually for the whole session. When in doubt, it's best to "shuffle" more and slow down.

FAT BURNING TRAINING: FOR THE REST OF YOUR LIFE

In this book you'll find a very successful fat burning training program for beginners. Once you have reached the end of this schedule, I have designed the following for continuing to do what you have started—and move to a higher level if you wish. The following is ideal, but many walkers don't have the time to do every component. I have assigned priorities next to each item.

[1] Top priority workouts—be sure to do these each week
[2] Second priority workouts—it would be very beneficial to do these each week
[3] Do these if you have time—they will help, just have a lower priority.

Days of the week are listed only as a suggestion. Feel free to adjust to your schedule. If you cannot do the total length of the session, do whatever you can—even 10 minutes is better than nothing. Walking is a great way to burn extra calories at any time (in the grocery store, parking farther away, etc.). Using a step counter will allow you to break up the walking into an all-day series of step segments. See the section below on 10,000 steps a day.

Sunday (1)

One longer walk (1). Start with the amount that you finished up with at the end of your introductory fat burning program and gradually increase to between 90 and 120 minutes. Once you reach the time that you want as your limit, you can adjust the walk-shuffle ratio, as you feel comfortable. Don't be afraid to put more shuffling in the beginning. The mission here is to keep going, while feeling good. You should finish knowing that you could have gone farther.

Monday (3)

An alternative exercise that raises body temperature, while allowing you to continue for 45+ minutes. Even on time-crunched days, try to shoot for 30 minutes. Even if you can only squeeze in 15 minutes, the extra calories burned will help in total fat burning for the week. Stair machine work is not recommended.

Tuesday (1)

A moderate walk of 40-60 minutes. These moderate walks allow you to maintain the fat-burning adaptations gained in the longer one on the weekend. These could be done at whatever pace you wish, but when in doubt—go slower— and go longer.

Wednesday (3)

Alternative exercise, same as Monday - 60 minutes

Thursday (1)

Same as Tuesday - 40-60 minutes

Friday (3)

Alternative exercise, same as Monday - 60 minutes

Saturday (3)

You can have this day off if you wish. Because it is the day before your long one, it's best to take it very easy if you do any exercise. A short and gentle walk would be fine, for example, but your top priority is having fresh muscles for Sunday's long one.

How much walking and how much shuffling?

Follow the guidelines in the "Shuffle" chapter, and "Getting Hooked On Walking" chapter. In the beginning, you may have to force yourself to shuffle—but if you do this, you will be able to go farther without getting as sore. Very gradually you will increase the amount of walking. Don't push too quickly. It would be better to choose a ratio that seems too easy for you.

10,000 or more steps a day

A pedometer, or step counter, can change your fat-burning life. This device gives you an incentive and reinforcement for adding extra steps to your day. It also gives you a great deal of control over your actual calorie burnoff. Once you get into the mind-set of taking more than 10,000 steps a day in your everyday activities, you find yourself getting out of your chair more often, parking farther away from the supermarket, walking around the kid's playground, etc.

Step counters are usually about one inch square, and clip onto your belt, pocket or waistband. The inexpensive models just count steps and this is all you need. Other models compute miles and calories. I recommend getting one from a quality manufacturer. When tested, some of the really inexpensive ones registered 3-4 times as many steps as the quality products did—walking exactly the same course.

Your goal is to accumulate more than 10,000 steps per day—at home, at work, going shopping, waiting for kids, etc. per day. This is very doable. You will find many pockets of time during the day when you are just sitting or standing. When you use these to add steps to your day, you burn fat and feel better. You become a very active person—and feel more energetic all day.

About dinnertime you should do a "step check." If you haven't acquired your 10,000, walk around the block a few extra times before/after dinner—and you don't have to stop there! As you get into it, you'll find many more opportunities to walk....and burn.

Up to 50 pounds of fat... gone!

Depending upon how many times you do the following each week, you have some opportunities each day to burn a little here, and a little there. These are easy movements that don't produce tiredness, aches or pains, but at the end of the year—it really adds up:

Pounds per year	Activity
1-2 pounds	taking the stairs instead of the elevator
3-10 pounds	getting out of your chair at work to walk down the hall
1-4 pounds	getting off the couch to move around the house (but not to get potato chips)
1-2 pounds	parking farther away from the supermarket, mall, etc
1-3 pounds	parking farther away from your work
2-4 pounds	walking around the kid's playground, practice field (chasing the kids)
2-4 pounds	walking up and down the concourse as you wait for your next flight (carpool, etc.)
3-9 pounds	walking the dog each day
2-4 pounds	walking a couple of times around the block after supper
2-4 pounds	walking a couple of times around the block during lunch hour at work
2-4 pounds	walking an extra loop around the mall, supermarket, etc. to look for bargains (this last one could be expensive when at the mall)

Total: 20-50 pounds a year

15 more pounds burned each year from adding a few extra miles a day

By using time periods when you usually have small pockets of time, you can add to your fat-burning without feeling extra fatigue:

- Slow down and go one more mile on each walk
- Walk a mile at lunchtime
- Walk a mile before dinner, or afterward or both

FAT BURNING: THE INCOME SIDE OF THE EQUATION

Gaining control over your calorie intake is crucial for body fat reduction. Walkers often complain that even though they have increased mileage, and have faithfully done their cross training workouts, they are not losing weight. In every case, when I have questioned them, each did not gain control over the amount of calories they were eating. In every case, when each went through the drill of quantifying, each was eating more than they thought. Below you will find ways to cut 10 or more pounds out of your diet—without starving yourself.

Websites give you control over calorie intake

The best tool I've found for managing your food intake is a good website or software program. There are a number of these that will help to document your calorie "balance sheet" (calories burned vs calories eaten). Your job is to log in your exercise for the day, and what you eat: food, quantity, condiments. At the end of the day, you can perform an accounting of calories, and of nutrients. If you are low on certain vitamins or minerals, protein, etc, after dinner, just eat the appropriate food or a vitamin pill. Some programs will tell vegetarians whether they have consumed enough complete protein, since this nutrient is harder to put together from vegetable sources. If you haven't met the minimum of any nutrient, you are empowered to do something about it that night, or the next morning to make up the deficit. If you ate too many calories, walk after dinner or boost tomorrow's workouts, or reduce the calories, or all of the above.

I don't recommend letting any website control your nutritional life until the end of your days. At first, it helps to power up the computer every day for 1-2 weeks. During this time, you'll see patterns, and note where you tend to fall short or over-eat. Every two weeks or so, do a spot check over 2-3 days. Some folks need more checks than others. If you're more motivated to eat the right foods and quantities by logging in every day, go for it.

For a list of the websites, see my website:

www.jeffgalloway.com

Try several out before you decide.

A portion of most foods is about the size of a fist

Portion control—through logging your food intake

Whether you use a website or not, the most important lesson is that of portion control. Bring a little note pad, and a small scale if you need it. Most folks who go through this drill for a week are surprised at the number of calories they are eating. The fat content is usually higher than estimated.

Many foods have the fat so well disguised that you don't realize how much you are eating until you look at the daily balance sheet.

You are gaining control!

After logging your food intake for several days you'll find yourself adjusting the amount that you eat at each meal. Many exercisers have told me that they resented the first week of logging in, but it became fairly routine after that. Once you get used to doing this, you become aware of what you will be putting in your mouth, and can take charge over your eating behaviors. This will allow you to burn the fat you want to burn.

Eating every 2 hours—can burn 8-10 pounds with no food reduction

As mentioned in the previous chapter, if you have not eaten for about 3 hours, your body senses that it is going into a starvation mode, and slows down the metabolism rate, while increasing the production of fat-depositing enzymes. This means that you will not be burning as many calories as is normal, that you won't be as mentally and physically alert, and that more of your next meal will be stored away as fat.

If the starvation reflex starts kicking in at about 3 hours, then you can beat it by eating every 2 hours. This is a great way to burn more calories. A person who now eats 2-3 times a day, can burn 8-10 pounds a year when they shift to 8-10 snacks/meals a day. This assumes that the same calories are eaten every day, in the same foods.

Big meals slow you down

Big meals are a big production for the digestive system. Blood is diverted to the long and winding intestine and the stomach. Because of the workload, the body tends to shut down blood flow to other areas, leaving you feeling more lethargic and sedentary—without the energy or blood flow to exercise well.

Small meals speed you up

Smaller amounts of food can usually be processed quickly without putting a burden on the digestive system. Each time you eat a small meal or snack, your metabolism speeds up. Faster metabolism, several times a day means calories burned.

You also give your set point... a setback

When you wait more than three hours between meals the set point engages the starvation reflex. But if you eat every 2-3 hours, the starvation reflex is not engaged—due to the regular supply of food. Therefore the fat depositing enzymes don't have to be stimulated.

Motivation increases when eating more often

The most common reason I've found for low motivation in the afternoon is not eating regularly enough during the day—especially during the afternoon. If you have not eaten for 4 hours or more, and you're scheduled for a walk that afternoon, you will not feel very motivated—because of low blood sugar and low metabolism. Even when you have had a bad eating day, and feel down in the dumps, you can gear up for a walk by having a snack 30-60 minutes before exercise. A fibrous energy bar with a cup of coffee (tea, diet drink) can reverse the negative mindset. By far the best strategy is to eat every 2-3 hours

Satisfaction from a small meal—to avoid overeating

The number of calories you eat per day can be reduced by choosing foods and combinations that leave you satisfied longer. Sugar is the worst problem in calorie control and satisfaction. When you drink a beverage with sugar in it, the sugar will be processed very quickly, and you'll often be hungry within 30 minutes—even after consuming a high quantity of calories. This will usually lead to two undesirable outcomes:

1. Eating more food to satisfy hunger
2. Staying hungry and triggering the starvation reflex

Your mission is to find the right combination of foods in your small meals that will leave you satisfied for 2-3 hours. Then eat another snack that will do the same. You will find a growing number of food combinations that may have a few more calories than your junk food snacks, but keep you from getting hungry for an hour or more.

Nutrients that leave you satisfied longer

Fat

Fat will leave you satisfied from a small meal because it slows down digestion, but a little goes a long way. When the fat content of a meal goes beyond 30%, you start to feel more lethargic due to the fact that fat is harder to digest. While up to about 18% of the calories in fat will help you hold hunger at bay, a lot of fat can compromise a fat-burning program. Fat is automatically deposited on your body. None of the fat in a snack is used for energy immediately. When you eat a fatty meal, you might as well inject it onto your hips or stomach. The fat you burn as fuel must be broken down from the stored fat on your body. So it helps to eat a little fat, but a lot of it will mean more fat on your body.

There are two kinds of fat that have been found to cause narrowing of the arteries around the heart and leading to your brain: saturated fat and trans fat. Mono and unsaturated fats from vegetable sources, are often healthy—olive oil, nuts, avocado, safflower oil. Some fish oils (from deep, coldwater fish) have Omega 3 fatty acids which have been shown to have a protective effect on the heart. Many fish have oil that is not protective, however, especially farm-fed fish.

Look carefully at the labels because a lot of foods have vegetable oils that have been processed into trans fat. A wide range of baked goods and other foods have trans fat. It helps to check the labels, and call the 800 number for foods that don't break down the fat composition—or avoid the food.

Protein—lean protein is best

This nutrient is needed every day for rebuilding the muscle that is broken down continuously, as well as from normal wear and tear. Even those who do miles of strenuous endurance exercise every day don't need to eat significantly more protein than sedentary people. But exercisers who don't get their usual amount of protein will feel more aches and pains, and general weakness sooner than average people.

Having protein with each meal will make you feel satisfied for a longer period of time. But eating more protein calories than you need will produce a conversion of the excess into fat.

Recently, protein has been added to sports drinks with great success. When a drink with 80% carbohydrate and 20% protein (such as Accelerade) is consumed within 30 minutes of the start of a walk, the stored sugar in your muscles is activated better, and energy is supplied sooner and better. By consuming a drink that has the same ratio (like Endurox R4) within 30 minutes of finishing a walk, you'll speed up the reloading of the muscles.

Complex carbohydrates give you a "discount" and a "grace period"

Foods such as celery, beans, cabbage, spinach, turnip greens, grape nuts, whole grain cereal, etc, require the body to burn up to 25% of the calories in digestion.

As opposed to fat (which is directly deposited on your body after eating it) it is only the excess carbs that are processed into fat. After dinner, for example, you have the opportunity to burn off any excess that you acquired during the day by getting on the treadmill or walking around the block.

Fat + Protein + Complex Carbs = SATISFACTION

Eating a snack that has a variety of the three satisfaction ingredients above, will lengthen the time that you'll feel satisfied—even after some very small meals. These three items take longer to digest, and therefore keep the metabolism rate revved up.

Other important nutrients...

Fiber

When fiber is put into foods, it slows down digestion and maintains the feeling of satisfaction longer. Soluble fiber, such as oat bran, seems to bestow a longer feeling of satisfaction than unsoluble fiber such as wheat bran. But any type of fiber will help in this regard.

Recommended percentages of the three nutrients:

There are differing opinions on this issue. Here are the ranges given by a number of top nutritionists that I have read and asked. These are listed in terms of the percentage per day of each of the calories consumed in each nutrient, compared to the total number of calories per day.

Protein:	between 18% and 28%
Fat:	between 15% and 25%
Carbohydrate:	whatever is left—hopefully in complex carbohydrates.

Simple Carbs help us put weight back on the body

The simple carbohydrates are too easy to eat. These are the "feel good" foods: candy, baked sweets, starches like mashed potatoes and rice, sugar drinks (including fruit juice and sports drinks) and most desserts. When you are on a fat burning mission, you need to minimize the amount of these foods.

The sugar in these products is digested so quickly that you get little or no lasting satisfaction from them. They often leave you with a craving for more of them, which, if denied, will produce a starvation reflex.

Because they are processed quickly, you become hungry relatively quickly and will eat again, accumulating extra calories that usually end up as fat at the end of the day.

As mentioned in the last chapter, it is never a good idea to eliminate them by saying "I'll never eat another...". This sets up a starvation reflex time bomb, ticking.

Keep taking a bite or two of the foods you dearly love, while cultivating the taste of foods with more fiber and little or no refined sugar or starch.

GOOD BLOOD SUGAR = MOTIVATION

The blood sugar level (BSL) determines how good you feel. When it is at a moderate, "normal" (for you) level—you feel good, stable and motivated. If you eat too much sugar, your BSL can rise too high. You'll feel really good for a while, but the excess sugar triggers a release of insulin, that usually pushes BSL too low. In this state your energy level drops, mental focus is foggy, and motivation goes down rapidly.

When blood sugar level is maintained throughout the day, you will be more motivated to exercise, and feel like adding other movement to your life. You'll have a more positive mental attitude, and be more likely to deal with stress and solve problems. Just as eating throughout the day keeps metabolism up, the steady infusion of balanced nutrients all day long will maintain stable blood sugar.

You don't want to get on the "bad side" of your BSL. Low levels are a stress on the system and literally mess with your mind. Your brain is fed by blood sugar and when the supply goes down, your mental stress goes up. If you have not eaten for several hours before a walk, you'll receive an

increase in the number of negative messages telling you don't have the energy to exercise, that it will hurt, and many others.

The simple act of eating a snack that has carbohydrate and about 20% protein will reduce the negative, make you feel good and get you out the door. Keeping a snack as a BSL booster can often be the difference whether you get out and walk that day, or not.

The BSL roller coaster

Eating a snack with too many calories of simple carbohydrate can be counter-productive for BSL maintenance. As mentioned above, when the sugar level gets too high, your body produces insulin, sending BSL lower than before. The tendency is to eat again, which produces excess calories that are converted into fat. But if you don't eat, you'll stay hungry and pretty miserable—in no mood to exercise or move around and burn calories or get in your walk for the day.

Eating every 2-3 hours is best

Once you find which snacks work best to maintain your BSL, most people maintain it better by eating small meals regularly, every 2-3 hours. As noted in the previous chapter, it's best to combine complex carbs with protein and a small amount of fat.

Do I have to eat before walking?

Only if your blood sugar is low. Most who walk in the morning don't need to eat anything before the start. As mentioned above, if your blood sugar level is low in the afternoon and you have a walk scheduled, a snack can help when taken about 30 minutes before the start. If you feel that a morning snack will help, the only issue is to avoid consuming so much that you get an upset stomach.

For best results in raising blood sugar when it is too low (within 30 minutes before a walk) a snack should have about 80% of the calories in simple carbohydrate and 20% in protein. This promotes the production of insulin which is helpful before exercise in getting the energy source (glycogen) in your muscles ready for use. The product Accelerade has worked best among the thousands of exercisers I hear from every year. It has the 80/20 ratio of carbohydrates to protein. If you eat an energy bar with the 80/20 ratio, be sure to drink 6-8 oz. of water with it.

Eating during exercise

Most exercisers don't need to worry about eating or drinking during a walk until the length of the session exceeds 90 minutes. At this point, there are several options. In each case, wait until you have been exercising for about 35 minutes before starting.

GU or Gel products—these come in small packets, and are the consistency of honey or thick syrup. The most successful way to take them is to put 1-2 packets in a small plastic bottle with a pop-top. About every 10-15 minutes, take 1-2 small squirts, with a sip or two of water

Energy Bars—cut into 8-10 pieces and take a piece, with a couple of sips of water, every 10-15 minutes.

Candy—particularly gummi bears or hard candies. The usual consumption is 1-2 about every 10 minutes.

Sports Drinks—Since there is significant percentage of nausea among those who drink during exercise, this is not my top recommendation. If you have found this to work for you, use it exactly as you have used it before—better to dilute it somewhat.

It is important to re-load after exercise—within 30 minutes

Whenever you have finished a hard or long workout (for you), a reloading snack will help you recover faster. Again, the 80/20 ratio of carb to protein has been most successful in reloading the muscles. The product that has worked best among the thousands I work with each year is Endurox R4.

AN ACTIVE PERSON'S DIET

A radical change in the foods you eat is not a good idea, and usually leads to problems. In this chapter, I will explain the items that are most important, and can help in maintaining good overall health and fitness.

As a regular exerciser you will not need significantly more vitamins and minerals, protein, etc than a sedentary person. But if you don't get these ingredients for several days in a row, you will feel the effects when you try to exercise.

Most important nutrient: water

Whether you take in your fluids in the form of water, juice or other fluids, drink regularly throughout the day. Under normal circumstances, your thirst is a good guide for fluid consumption. I will not tell you that you must drink 8 glasses of water a day, because I've not seen any research to back this up. Fluid researchers who follow this topic tell me that the research says that if we drink regularly and when thirsty, fluid levels are replaced fairly quickly.

If you are needing bathroom stops during walks, you are usually drinking too much—either before or during the exercise. During an exercise session of 60 minutes or less, most exercisers don't need to drink at all. The intake of fluid before exercise should be arranged so that the excess amount is eliminated before the walk. Each person is a bit different, so you will have to find a routine that works for you. In other words, you'll have to get your timing down on your pre-exercise drinking.

Even during extremely long ones of over 4 hours, medical experts from major marathons recommend no more than 27 oz an hour of fluid. Most folks need much less than this.

Sweat the electrolytes

Electrolytes are the salts that your body loses when you sweat: sodium, potassium, magnesium and calcium. When these minerals get too low, your fluid transfer system doesn't work as well and you may experience ineffective cooling, swelling of the hands, and other problems. Most walkers have no problem replacing these in a normal diet, but if you are experiencing cramping during or after exercise, regularly, you may be low in sodium or potassium.

The best product I've found for replacing these minerals is called SUCCEED. If you have high blood pressure, get your doctor's guidance before taking any salt supplement.

Practical eating issues

- You don't need to eat before a walk, unless your blood sugar is low (see the previous chapter)
- Reload most effectively by eating within 30 min of the finish of a walk (80% carb/20% protein)
- Eating or drinking too much right before the start of a walk will interfere with deep breathing, & may cause side pain. The food or fluid in your stomach, limits your intake of air into the lower lungs, and increases the chance of side pain.
- If you are running low on blood sugar at the end of your long ones, take some blood sugar booster with you (see the previous chapter for suggestions)
- It is never a good idea to eat a huge meal. Those who claim that they must "carbo load" are rationalizing the desire to eat a lot of food. Eating a big meal the night before (or the day of) a long walk can be a real problem. You will have a lot of food in your gut, and you will be bouncing up and down for an extended period. Get the picture?

When you are sweating a lot, it is a good idea to drink several glasses a day (1-2 hours apart) of a good electrolyte beverage. Accelerade, by Pacific Health Labs, is the best I've seen for both maintaining fluid levels and electrolyte levels.

Exercise Eating Schedule

- 1 hour before a morning walk: either a cup of coffee or a glass of water
- 30 minutes before any walk (if blood sugar is low) about 100 calories of Acclerade
- Within 30 minutes after a walk: about 200 calories of a 80% carb/20% protein (Endurox R4, for example)
- If you are sweating a lot during hot weather, 6-12 oz. of a good electrolyte beverage like Accelerade, about every 1-2 hours—during the periods of the day when you are not exercising—as well as when you are walking.

Meal Ideas

Breakfast Options

1. Whole grain bread made into French toast with fruit yogurt, juice, or frozen juice concentrate as syrup
2. Whole grain pancakes with fruit and yogurt
3. A bowl of Grape Nuts cereal, skim milk, non fat yogurt, and fruit

Lunch Options

1. Tuna fish sandwich, whole grain bread, a little low fat mayo, cole slaw (with fat free dressing)
2. Turkey breast sandwich with salad, low fat cheese, celery & carrots
3. Veggie burger on whole grain bread, low fat mayo, salad of choice

4. Spinach salad with peanuts, sunflower seeds, almonds, low fat cheese, non fat dressing, whole grain rolls or croutons

Dinner Options

There are lots of great recipes in publications such as COOKING LIGHT. The basics are listed below. What makes the meal come alive are the seasonings which are listed in the recipes. You can use a variety of fat substitutes.

1. Fish or lean chicken breast or tofu (or other protein source) with whole wheat pasta, and steamed vegetables
2. Rice with vegetables, and a protein source
3. Dinner salad with lots of different vegetables, nuts, lean cheese or turkey, or fish, or chicken

I recommend Nancy Clark's books. Her Sports Nutrition Guidebook is a classic.

NO ACHES, NO PAINS, NO INJURIES

$\mathbf{B}$ecause walking is a survival activity from the primitive beginnings of man, almost everyone has inherited all of the capabilities and potential adaptations to walk for long distances. Most walkers develop a balance of stress and rest, with gentle increases, so they continue to improve without injury. In fact, the single greatest reason for fitness improvement is *not getting injured*.

But inside each human is a personality trait that can compromise this progression. I call this the "Type A over-exerciser syndrome." Even those who feel they have no competitive urges and no athletic background need to be on guard. Once a new walker has achieved a certain level of fitness, there is a tendency to increase more or rest less. At first, the body responds. But at some point, continued stress builds up on certain "weak links", producing injury.

Watch out for the weak links

Each of us has a very few areas that take on more stress, and tend to produce most of the aches, pains and injuries. The most common areas are the knees, the foot, the shins, and the hip. Those who have been walking for a year or more will usually know these areas. If you have a particular place on your knee that has been hurt before, and it hurts after a long walk, take an extra day or two off, and follow the suggestions on treating an injury, listed below.

Am I really injuried?

The following are the leading signs that you have an injury. If you feel any of the three below, you should stop your workout immediately and take some extra rest days (usually 2-3). Trying to walk through an injury, in the early stages, creates a dramatically worse injury—even on one walk. If you take 2-3 days off at the first symptom, you may avoid having to stop exercise for 2-3 months when trying to push through it. It is always safer to err on the side of taking more time off, when pain is concerned.

Signs of Injury

1. Inflammation—any type of swelling
2. Loss of function—the foot, etc, doesn't work correctly
3. Pain—that does not go away when you "shuffle" for a few minutes

How fast will I lose my conditioning?

Studies have shown that you can maintain conditioning even when you don't exercise for 5 days. Surely you want to continue regular walking if you can, but staying injury free has an even higher priority. So don't be afraid to take up to 5 days off when a "weak link" kicks in. In most cases you will only stop for 2-3 days.

Treatment

It is always best, at the first sign of injury, to see a doctor (or with muscle injury—a massage therapist) who wants to get you out there exercising as soon as possible. The more responsive doctors will explain what they believe is wrong (or tell you when he/she cannot come up with a diagnosis) and give you a treatment plan. This will give you great confidence in the process, which has been shown to speed the healing.

What you can do while waiting for the doctor

Unfortunately, most of the better doctors are so booked up that it's difficult to get an appointment. While waiting, here are some things other walkers have done with success when one of the weak links shows inflammation, loss of function or pain:

1. Take at least 2-5 days off from any activity that could irritate it
2. If the injured area is next to the skin (tendon, foot, etc), rub a chunk of ice on the area(s)—constantly rubbing for 15 minutes, until it gets numb. Continue to do this for a week after you feel no symptoms.
3. If the problem is inside a joint or muscle, call your doctor and ask if you can use prescription strength anti-inflammatory medication. Don't take any medication without a doctor's advice—and follow that advice.
4. If you have a muscle injury, see a very successful sports massage therapist. Try to find one who has a lot of successful experience treating the area where you are injured. The magic fingers and hands can often work wonders.

Preventing injury—everyone's goal

Although I didn't count them all, I know I have suffered over a hundred injuries during my exercise career. Plus I have worked with tens of thousands who have also had to work through aches and pains, so I've developed the suggestions below. They are based upon my experience, one exerciser to another. I'm proud to report that since I started following the advice that I give others, I've not had an overuse injury in over 25 years.

The 48-hour magical break

Allowing the walking muscles to rest the day after a strenuous walk will provide a magic time period for recovery. Stair machine work should also be avoided during the 48-hour rest period (stair work uses the same muscles as walking).

No stretching allowed!

I've come full circle on this. A high percentage of the exercisers who report injuries to me have either become injured because they stretched or aggravated the injury by stretching. When they stop stretching, a significant percentage report that the injury heals enough to walk in a relatively short period of time. The exception to this rule is when you have ilio-tibial band injury. For this injury alone, stretching the IT band seems to help walkers continue to walk, while they heal.

Do the "toe squincher" exercise

This exercise can be done 10-30 times a day, on both feet (one at a time). Point the toes and squinch them until the foot cramps (only a few seconds). This strengthens the many little muscles in the foot that can provide a platform of support. It is particularly effective in preventing plantar fascia.

Limit your increase in total mileage to 10% per week

Monitor your mileage that you walk in a log book or calendar. If you exceed the 10 per cent increase on a given week, take an extra day off.

Every third or fourth week, reduce your total mileage by 25%—even when increasing by no more than 10% per week. Your log book can guide you here also. You won't lose any conditioning and you'll help the body heal itself, and get stronger. A steady increase, week after week, does not allow the legs to catch up and rebuild.

Stick with the short stride

Walking with more of a shuffle (feet close to the ground) reduces the chance of many injuries. Walking with a long stride can irritate the shin muscles. Read the "walking form" section for more information on developing an efficient and smooth technique.

WALKING FORM: MAINTAINING MOMENTUM

Most walkers walk efficiently and correctly. In general, if you feel comfortable, with the least amount of pounding on your feet or tension on leg muscles or tendons—you're doing it right. Walkers tend to get off track when they try to imitate others, or walk faster than is natural for them by lengthening the stride. In this chapter we'll start with the basics, and then get into specific areas of the body. In this way, you can go right to the body part or problem area that gives you trouble.

Both in running and walking, very little strength is needed to move forward. The first few strides get you into motion, and your mission then becomes simple: to stay in motion. To reduce fatigue, aches and pains, your body intuitively fine-tunes your momentum so that you minimize effort as you continue to walk. Long walks are the best "lab" for you to make the adaptations listed below to walk easier. But it is also important to maintain these mechanics—with by regular walks, about every other day.

Humans have many bio-mechanical adaptations, which have been made more efficient over a period of more than a million years of walking. The prime source of this efficiency in humans is based upon the use of the ankle and the Achilles tendon. This extremely sophisticated system of levers, springs, balancing devices, and more involves hundreds of component parts and is amazingly well coordinated and effective.

When we walk, a very little amount of effort from the calf muscle produces a smooth continuation of forward movement. As the calf muscle gets in better shape and improves endurance, you can keep going mile after mile with little perceived effort. Other muscle groups offer support and fine-tune the process. When you feel aches and pains that might be due to the way you walk, going back to the minimal use of the ankle and Achilles tendon can often leave you feeling smooth and efficient very quickly.

Overview of walking form

Walking at a gentle, strolling pace produces few problems. But every year a small percentage of walkers get injured because they move outside their natural range of motion, and aggravate some area of the foot or leg. Most of these problems come from trying to walk too fast, with too long a stride, or from using a race walking or power walking technique.

1. *Avoid a long walking stride.* Maintain a relaxed, motion that does not stress the knees, tendons or muscles of the leg, feet, knees or hips. If you feel pain or aggravation in these areas, shorten your stride. Many beginners find that they can learn to walk fairly fast with a short stride. But when in doubt, walk with a shorter stride.

2. *Don't lead with your arms.* Minimal arm swing is best. Swinging the arms too much can encourage a longer walk stride which can push into aches and pains quickly. Arm swing rotation can also aggravate hips, shoulder and neck areas. You want the legs to set the rhythm for your walk. When this happens you are more likely to get into the "zone" of the right brain.

3. *Let your feet move the way that is natural for them.* When walkers try techniques that supposedly increase stride length by landing further back on the heel or pushing further on the toe than the legs are designed to move, many get injured.

Note: I will not cover the walking techniques of "race walking" or "power walking". These specialized ways of walking force the body to move in ways it is not designed for and produce many injuries.

A better way of walking?

There may be a better way to walk for you, one that will leave your legs with more strength and fewer aches and pains. The fact is, however, that most walkers are not far from optimal efficiency. I believe this is due to the action of the right brain. After tens of thousands of steps, it keeps searching for (and then refining) the most efficient pattern of movement, and alignment of feet, legs, and body.

In my weekend retreats, I conduct an individual form analysis with each person. After having analyzed over 10 thousand exercisers, I've also found that most are moving in a very efficient way. The problems are seldom big ones—but one or more small mistakes. By making a few minor adjustments, most walkers can feel better on every walk.

The big three problem areas: posture, stride, and bounce
I've discovered through these consultations that when walkers have problems they tend to occur in three areas: Posture, stride, and bounce. And the problems tend to be very individual, occurring most often in specific areas, because of specific motions. It is the repetitive abuse that comes from long walks with form irregularities that produces the aches and pains due to form. Slight over-stride, for example, creates fatigue and then weakness at the end of a walk. As a tired body "wobbles", other muscle groups try to keep the body on course, but are not designed for this, becoming overwhelmed.

The big three negative results (of inefficient form):

1. Fatigue becomes so severe that it takes much longer to recover

2. Muscles are pushed so far beyond their limits that they break down and become injured.

3. The experience is so negative, that the desire to walk is reduced, producing burnout.

Almost everyone has some slight problem. I don't suggest that everyone should try to create perfect form. But when you become aware of your form problems, and make changes to keep them from producing aches and pains, you'll feel fewer pains, smoother motion, and walk faster (if you want). This chapter can help you understand why aches and pains tend to come out of form problems—and how you may be able to reduce or eliminate them.

How to check your own form

In some of my clinics, I use a digital camera that gives instant feedback. If you have one of these cameras, have a friend take pictures of you walking, from the side (not walking towards or away from the camera) while you walk on a flat surface. Some walkers can check themselves while walking alongside stores that offer a reflection in a plate glass window—especially if the glass goes all the way to the sidewalk. Seeing yourself walk on a video screen is much better. The sections below will tell you what to look for.

How do you feel? The best test

If you feel relaxed and walking is easy—you're probably walking correctly. Overall, the walking motion should feel easy. There should be no tension in your neck, back, shoulders or legs. A good way to correct problems is to change posture, foot or leg placement, etc, so that you feel smoother, with less effort.

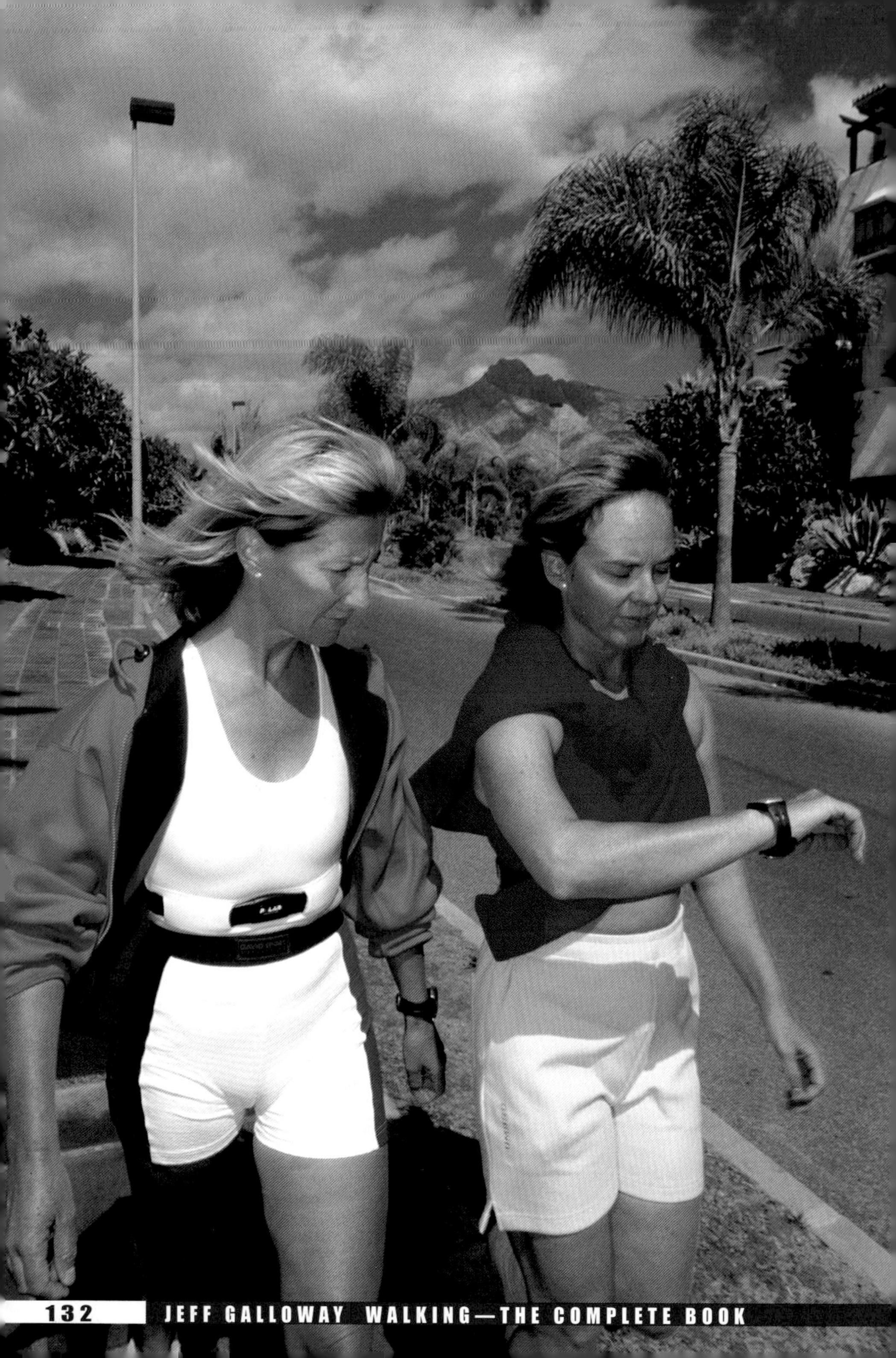

Posture—it's about balance and alignment

Good walking posture is actually good body posture. The head is naturally balanced over the shoulders, which are aligned over the hips. As the foot comes underneath, all of these elements are in balance so that no energy is needed to prop up the body. You shouldn't have to work to pull a wayward body back from a wobble or inefficient motion.

Error: Forward lean

The posture errors tend to be mostly due to a forward lean—especially when we are tired. The head wants to get finished as soon as possible, but the legs can't go any faster. At the end of tiring long ones, walkers will often lean so far that the heads are literally ahead of the body. If you've pushed yourself to the limit, a forward lean can mean falling, or tripping over the slightest pebble on the road. A forward lean will often concentrate fatigue, soreness and tightness in the lower back, or neck.

It all starts with the head. When the neck muscles are relaxed, the head is usually in a natural position. If there is tension in the neck, or soreness afterward, the head is usually leaning too far forward. This triggers a more general upper body imbalance in which the head and chest are suspended slightly ahead of the hips and feet. Ask a walking companion to tell you if and when your head is too far forward, or leaning down. The ideal position of the head is mostly upright, with your eyes focused about 30-40 yards ahead of you.

Error: Sitting back

The hips are the other major postural area where walkers can get out of alignment. A walker with this problem, when observed from the side, will have the butt behind the rest of the body. When the pelvis area is shifted back, the legs are not allowed to go through a natural range of motion, and the stride length becomes artificially short. Hips and thigh muscles and tendons experience more aches and pains when this is the case. This produces a slower pace, even when spending significant effort. Many walkers tend to hit harder on their heels when their hips are shifted back—producing heel pain afterward

Error: Backward lean (rare)

It is rare for walkers to lean back, but it happens. In my experience, this is usually due to a structural problem in the spine or hips. If you do this, and you're having pain in the neck, back or hips, you should see a doctor.

Postural Correction: "Puppet on a string"

The best correction I've found to postural problems has been this mental exercise: imagine that you are a puppet on a string. Suspended from up above like a puppet—from the head and each side of the shoulders—your head lines up above the shoulders, the hips come directly underneath, and the feet naturally touch lightly. It won't hurt anyone to do the "puppet" several times during a walk.

It helps to combine this image with a deep breath. About every 4-5 minutes, as you take a good (lower lung) breath, straighten up and say "I'm a puppet." Then imagine that you don't have to spend energy maintaining this upright posture, because the strings attached from above keep you on track. As you continue to do this, you reinforce good posture and work on making this behavior a habit.

Upright posture not only allows you to stay relaxed, you will probably improve your stride length. When you lean forward, you'll tend to cut your stride to stay balanced. When you straighten up, you'll receive a stride bonus of an inch or so, without any increase in energy. When this happens, it should occur naturally—don't try to extend your stride.

An oxygen dividend

Breathing improves when you straighten up. A leaning body can't get ideal use out of the lower lungs. This can cause side pain. When you walk upright, the lower lungs can receive adequate air, absorb the oxygen better, and all of this reduces the chance of side pain.

No more bounce—Feet low to the ground

The most efficient stride is a shuffle—with feet right next to the ground. As long as you pick your foot up enough to avoid stumbling over a rock or uneven pavement, stay low to the ground. Most walkers don't need to get more than 1" clearance.

Your ankle combined with your Achilles tendon will act as a spring, moving you forward on each walking step. If you stay low to the ground, very little effort is required. Through this efficient technique, each step comes almost automatic. When walkers err on bounce, they try to push off too hard. This usually results in extra effort spent in lifting the body off the ground—and soreness in the muscles or joints. Think of this as energy wasted in the air—energy that could be used to walk another mile or two.

The other negative force that penalizes a higher bounce is that of gravity. The higher you rise, the harder you will fall. Each additional bounce off the ground delivers a lot more impact on feet and legs—which on long walks produces aches, pains and injuries. Extra bounce in walking can aggravate the tendons in the ankle.

The correction for too much bounce: Light touch

The ideal foot placement should be so light that you don't usually feel yourself pushing off or landing. This means that your foot stays low to the ground and goes though an efficient and natural motion. Instead of trying to overcome gravity, you get in synch with it.

Stride length – often the culprit

After analyzing thousands, I've come to the conclusion that the key to faster and more efficient walking is increased cadence or turnover of feet and legs.

A major cause of aches, pains and injuries is a stride length that is too long. At the end of this chapter you'll see a list of problems and how to correct them. When in doubt, it is always better to err on the side of having a shorter stride.

Don't lift your knees!

A high knee lift tires the quadracep muscle (front of the thigh), leading to a stride that is too long to be efficient. The most common time when walkers stride too long is at the end of a tiring walk. This slight overstride when the legs are tired will leave your quads (front of thigh) sore the next day or two.

Don't kick out too far in front of you!

If you watch the natural movement of the leg, it will kick forward slightly as the foot gently moves forward in the walking motion to contact the ground. Let this be a natural motion that produces no tightness in the muscles behind the lower or upper leg.

Tightness in the front of the shin, or behind the knee, or in the hamstring (back of the thigh) is a sign that you are kicking too far forward, and reaching out too far. Correct this by staying low to the ground, shortening the stride, and lightly touching the ground.

Cadence or turnover drill

This drill helps to pull all the elements of good walking form together at the same time. Over the weeks and months, if you do this drill once every week, you will find that your normal cadence slowly increases naturally as you develop an efficient movement of the foot and leg.

1. Warm up by walking very slowly for 5 minutes, and then shuffling and walking very gently for 10 minutes.

2. Start by walking faster—to a normal pace for 1-2 minutes, and then time yourself for 30 seconds. During this half minute, count the number of times your left foot touches.

3. Shuffle around, or walk gently, for a minute or so.

4. On the next 30 second drill, increase the count by 1 or 2.

5. Repeat this 3-7 more times. Each time trying to increase by 1-2 additional counts.

In the process of improving turnover, the body's internal monitoring system coordinates a series of adaptations which pulls together all of the form components into an efficient team:

- Your foot touches more gently, yet quickly and with a light touch
- Extra, inefficient motions of the foot and leg are reduced or eliminated
- Less effort is spent on pushing up or pushing forward
- You stay lower to the ground
- The ankle becomes more efficient
- Ache and pain areas are not overused

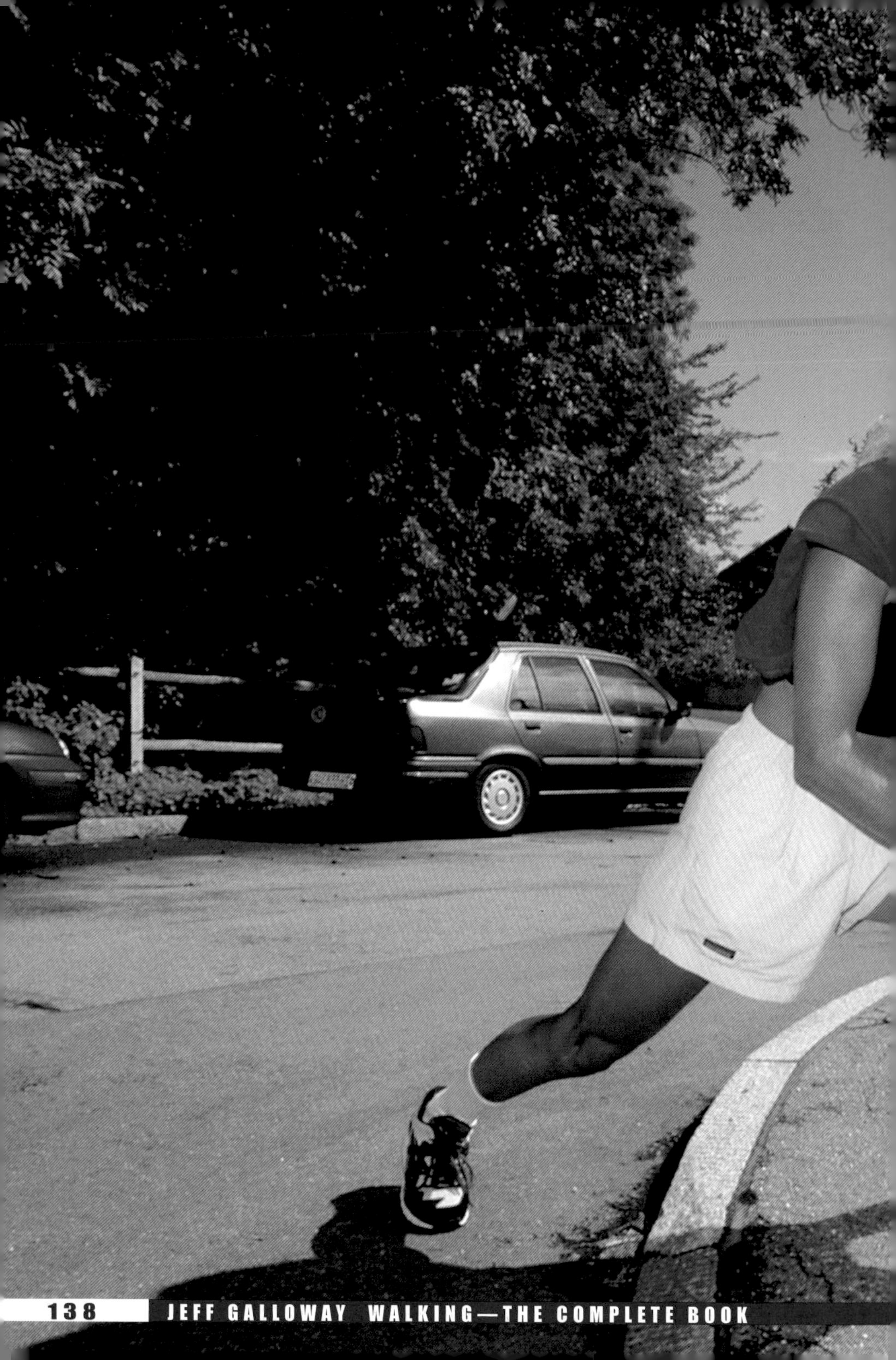

STRETCHING

Stretching causes injuries. Does that surprise you? It may, because it is totally at odds with what we have heard from exercise gurus for so many years. But my surveys have found that among those who stretch regularly, stretching is the leading cause of injury. While there are some specific stretches that help some individuals, I believe that most people who walk don't need to stretch at all. I know that you will get a lot of advice to stretch—especially from those who are involved in other activities like tennis, swimming, soccer, golf, etc. Walking is significantly different than those other activities.

In other sports, you are asking your body to do what it was not designed to do. Our ancient ancestors didn't play tennis or golf. But they did walk. If we walk gently, as noted in this book, we will stay within the ranges of motion for which we were designed. Stretching pushes the tendons and muscles beyond what they are currently ready to do, and often produces an injury.

What about tightness?

Don't be alarmed by a slight increase in tightness of the leg muscles as you increase your distance. On an individual walk, most of the tightness comes from muscle fatigue and the waste products that are deposited as you continue. Stretching will not take away this type of tightness.

A false sense of relief I fully admit that if you stretch a tired, tight muscle, it feels better…for a short period. After talking to dozens of physiologists, orthopedists, and other specialists, I've come to understand that stretching a tight muscle results in many small tears of the muscle fibers. Your body senses this and sends hormones to kill the pain—allowing the area to feel better, but only temporarily. But even one stretch under these conditions can injure a muscle and definitely increases recovery time as your body repairs the stretching damage. Even with light stretching, you will stress and weaken the muscle.

Some tightness is good Your body will get a bit tighter as you walk, for a while. This is due to the legs adapting to make distance walking more efficient: Your push from the foot becomes more effective and your range of motion more efficient. I've been told by many biomechanics experts that this type of tightness, in most cases, reduces the chance of injury and makes walking easier.

If you are having a problem with tightness in a certain part of the body, massage can help—even using the self help massage tools, such as "the stick."

Yoga and Pilates?

I communicate with exercisers every week who get injured because they stretched during these programs. Even mild stretches that are outside your range of motion can be adverse to the joints and tendons. The philosophical benefits of Yoga can be as significant as those from walking. If you benefit from such mental benefits go through the sessions—but don't stretch.

Ilio-tibial band injury—the only major exception

The ilio-tibial is a band of fascia that acts as a tendon. It starts at the hip and continues along the outside of each leg, attaching in several places below the knee. Besides the stretch noted here, individuals find that there are specific stretches that will help to release the tightness of their I-T band. Those who suffer from this injury can stretch before,

after, or during a walk, or whenever it tightens up and/or starts to hurt. There is more on this injury in the injury section of this book.

It's OK not to stretch before you walk

A gentle walk for 5 minutes, followed by a very gradual transition from slow walking to shuffle/walk has been the most effective warm up I have found.

Some stretches may work for you ... DO THEM!

I've met several people who have certain stretches that seem to help them. If you find a stretch that works for you, go ahead. Just be careful.

STRENGTHENING

As noted in the "walking form" chapter, walking is done most effectively in my opinion, by using your momentum. In other words, it's an "inertia activity." Once you get your body into motion with a few steps, just maintain that momentum. Minimal strength is required. There are a few strengthening activities that can help your walking—especially postural exercises. But I must tell you that overall, I don't believe that walking is a strength activity. With these facts on the table, it won't surprise you that this chapter is quite short.

Below are some exercises that I have found to help build strength that has reduced injury and increased walking efficiency. These are not meant to be prescriptions for medical problems. They are offered from one exerciser to another because thousands have reported benefit from them. If you have a back or other medical issue, make sure your doctor and other specialists give you permission to use these exercises.

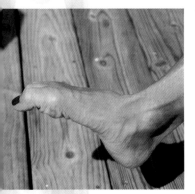

Toe squincher—for prevention of injuries of the foot and lower leg

I believe that this exercise will help every person that walks. Whether barefooted or not, point your toes and contract the muscles of your foot until they cramp. It only takes a few seconds for this to happen. You can repeat this exercise 10-30 times a day, every day.

This is the best way I know to prevent a foot injury called plantar fascia—but it strengthens the areas all over the foot and ankle for better support. I've also heard from exercisers who believe it has helped to prevent Achilles tendon problems.

Postural muscle exercises

By balancing the strength of muscles on the upper body that support your posture, you'll tend to maintain positive upright posture while walking, and in other of life's activities. In the upright position that is natural for you, walking is easier. You'll move forward more efficiently with less energy required for keeping your body balanced.

Good postural muscles will also allow for more efficient breathing. You'll be able to breathe deeply, which will reduce side pain and enable you to maximize oxygen absorption.

There are two groups of muscles that need to be strengthened. On the front side, the abdominal group provides support and balance. When this "ab" strength is balanced by back and neck muscles, you will resist fatigue in the shoulders, neck, and back.

Front muscles: the crunch

Lie on your back, on a cushioned carpet or floor pad with adequate cushioning for your back. Bend your knees. Now raise your head and upper back very slightly off the floor. Go up an inch or two and down, but don't let the upper back hit the floor. As you move very slightly, don't let the stomach muscles relax—keep them working as you go up and down in this very narrow range of motion. It also helps, as you are doing this, to roll slightly to either side, continuously moving. This strengthens the whole range of muscle groups that support the front side of your torso.

For the back, shoulders and neck: arm running

Holding a dumbbell in each hand, while standing (not while walking), go through a range of motion that you would use when walking or running. Keep the weights close to your body, as the hands swing from your waist up to your shoulders, and return.

Pick a weight that makes you feel, after a set of 10 repetitions, that you received a workout. But don't have so much weight that you have to struggle as you get your last 1-2 reps. Start with one set of 10, and increase to 3-5 sets, once or twice a week. This can be done on a walking day, or on a rest day.

Prescriptive exercises

These are designed for those who feel that they need more support in one or more of the areas listed below. Those walkers who have had regular aches, pains or injuries in one of the areas below have received benefit from these exercises.

Knees—the stiff leg lift

If you have knees that ache regularly, here is an exercise that strengthens the various muscles in the thigh. By developing strength in the range of muscles above, you may tighten the connections around the knee getting better support. When this group, the quadriceps, has more strength, and you keep your foot in a small range of motion directly below the hips, the knee takes less stress.

Sit on a tall bench or table. With a stiff leg, lift the leg up and down, gradually changing the range of motion from inside to outside. Start with no weight, and one set of 10 lifts. When you can easily do 3 sets of 10 lifts with each leg, add a few pounds using a bag or pocketbook looped around the ankle.

Shins—2 exercises

The foot lift

Sit on a bench, with knee bent at a right angle. Your foot must be significantly off the floor. Hang a bag or pocket book with a pound of weight over the foot. Lift your foot up and down 10 times. Move the angle of the foot to the inside and the outside. Add more weight when several sets of 10 feel easy.

Heel walking

Use a very padded shoe. Walk on your heels so that your toe region is off the floor. Start with 10 steps, and increase until you can do 2-3 sets of 20-30 steps.

HOW TO STAY
MOTIVATED

- Consistency is the most important part of conditioning and fitness
- Motivation is the most important factor in being consistent
- You can gain control over your motivation—every day

The choice is yours. You can take control over your attitude, or you can let yourself be swayed by outside factors that will leave you on a motivational roller coaster: fired up one day, and down the next. Getting motivated on a given day can sometimes be as simple as saying a few key words and taking a walk. But staying motivated requires a strategy or motivational training program. To understand the process, we must first look inside your head.

The brain has two hemispheres that are separated and don't interconnect. The logical left-brain does our business activities, trying to steer us into pleasure and away from discomfort. The creative and intuitive right side is an unlimited source of solutions to problems and connects us to hidden strengths.

As we accumulate stress, the left-brain sends us a stream of logical messages that tell us "you don't need to exercise today," "you've got so much to do," "this isn't your day," and even philosophical messages like "why are you doing this." We are all capable of staying on track, and maintaining motivation even when the left-brain is saying these things.

So the first important step in taking command over motivation is to ignore the left-brain unless there is a legitimate reason of health or safety (very rare). You can deal with the left-brain through a series of mental training drills.

These drills allow the right side of the brain to work on solutions to the problems you are having. As the negative messages spew out of the left-brain, the right-brain doesn't argue—it just goes to work, solving problems. By preparing mentally for the challenges you expect, you will empowered to deal with the problems and to develop mental toughness. But even more important, you will gain confidence from just having a strategy comprised of proven ways of dealing with the problems.

Rehearsing Success

Getting out the door after a hard day

By rehearsing yourself through a motivation problem, you can be more consistent and set the stage to improve. You must first have a goal that is do-able, and a rehearsal situation that is realistic. Let's learn by doing:

1. State your desired outcome: To be walking from my house after a hard day
2. Detail the challenge: Low blood sugar and fatigue, a stream of negative messages, need to get the evening meal ready to be cooked, overwhelming desire to feel relaxed
3. Break up the challenge into a series of actions which lead you through the mental barriers, no one of which is challenging to the left-brain.
   - You're driving home at the end of the day, knowing that it is a scheduled exercise day but you have no energy
   - Your left-brain says: "You're too tired," "take the day off," "You don't have the energy to walk"
   - So you say to the left-brain: "I'm not going to exercise. I'll put on some comfortable shoes and

clothes, eat and drink, get food preparation going for dinner, and feel relaxed."

- You're in your room, putting on comfortable clothes and shoes (they just happen to be used for walking)
- You're drinking coffee (tea, diet cola, etc.) and eating a good tasting energy snack, as you get the food prepared to go into the oven.
- Stepping outside, you check on the weather
- You're walking out to the edge of your block to see what the neighbors are doing
- As you cross the street, you're on your way
- The endorphins are kicking in, you feel good, you want to continue

4. Rehearse the situation over and over, fine-tuning it so that it becomes integrated into the challenges of your life and is in "synch" with the way you think and act.

5. Enjoy the reward. Finish by mentally focusing on the good feelings experienced with the desired outcome. You have felt the good attitude, the vitality, the glow from a good walk, and you are truly relaxed. So revisit these positive feelings at the end of each rehearsal.

Getting out the door early in the morning

The second most common motivational problem that I'm asked about relates to the comfort of the bed, when you wake up and know that it is time for exercise.

State your desired outcome: To be walking away from the house early in the morning

Detail the challenge: Desire to lie in bed, no desire to exert yourself so early. The stress of the alarm clock, and having to think about what to do next when the brain isn't working very fast.

Break up the challenge into a series of actions which lead you through the mental barriers, no one of which is challenging to the left-brain.

- The night before, you lay out your walking clothes and shoes, near your coffee pot, so that you don't have to think.
- Set your alarm, and say to yourself over and over: "alarm off, feet on the floor, to the coffee pot," or…."alarm, floor, coffee." As you repeat this, you visualize doing each action without thinking. By repeating it, you lull yourself to sleep. You have been programming yourself for taking action the next morning.
- The alarm goes off. You shut it off, put feet on the floor, and you head to the coffee pot—all without thinking.
- You're putting on one piece of clothing at a time, sipping coffee, never thinking about exercise.
- With coffee cup in hand, you walk out the door to see what the weather is like.
- Sipping coffee you walk to edge of your block or property to see what the neighbors are doing.
- Putting coffee down, you cross the street, and you have made the break!
- The endorphins are kicking in, you feel good, you want to continue.

Rehearsals become patterns of behavior more easily if you don't think but just move from one action to the next. The power of the rehearsal is that you have formatted your brain for a series of actions so that you don't have to think as you move from one action to the next. As you repeat the pattern, revising it for real life, you become what you want to be. You are successful!

DESTROYING
EXCUSES

All of us have days when we don't feel like exercising. On some of those days you probably need a day off, due to sickness or too much physical activity. But usually this is not the case.

The fact is that when we are under stress in life (and who isn't) the left brain will have dozens of great reasons why we shouldn't walk. They are all perfectly logical and accurate.

Each of us can choose whether to listen to the excuse or not. Once you quickly decide whether there is a medical (or other legitimate reason) why you shouldn't walk, most of the time you'll conclude that the left brain is just trying to make you lazy.

Thinking ahead will not take any significant time away from your day, and will destroy most of these excuses. You'll discover pockets of time, more energy, quality time with kids, and more enjoyment of exercise than you thought were possible for you.

The following is a list of excuses that most of us hear on a regular basis. With each, I've given a strategy for breaking through the excuse. Most of the time, it is as simple as just getting out there.

But overall, you are the captain of your ship. If you take charge over your schedule and your attitude, you will plan ahead. As you learn to ignore the left brain, and put one foot in front of the other, the endorphins start flowing, and the excuses start to melt away.

Life is good!

I don't have time to walk

Most of the recent US Presidents have been regular exercisers, as well as most of their Vice-Presidents. Are you busier than the President? There are always pockets of time, 5 minutes here, 10 minutes there, when you can insert a walk. With planning, you'll find several half-hours each day. Many walkers find that as they get in better shape, they don't need as much sleep, which allows for a chunk of time before the day gets started. It all gets down to the question "Are you going to take control over the organization of your day or not?" Once you look at your schedule, you'll usually discover other time blocks that allow you to do other things. By making time for a walk, you will also tend to be more productive and efficient, more than "paying back" the time you spend. Bottom line is that you have the time—seize it and you will have more quality in your life.

The walk will make me tired

If this happens, you are the one responsible. You have almost complete control over this situation. By going at a conservative pace, with the right amount of shuffling, you will feel better and more energized than before you started. If you have a bad habit of pushing the pace too much in the beginning, then get control over yourself! Walk very slowly in the beginning, and shuffle even more. As you learn to slow down, you'll be able to go farther with more energy.

I need to spend some time with my kids

There are a number of exercise strollers that allow parents to walk with their kids. My wife and I logged thousands of miles with our first child in single "baby jogger." We got a twin carrier after our second was born. With the right pacing, you can talk to the kids about anything, and they can't run or crawl away. Sorry, they don't have a model for teenagers. Because you are with the kid(s) in close company, we found that we talked more, and got more feedback than doing other activities together. By bringing them along with you on a walk, you become a great role model: even though busy, you take time to exercise and spend time together.

I've got too much work to do

There will always be work to do. Several surveys have found that exercisers get more work done on days they work out. Walking produces more energy and a better attitude. It reduces stress. Hundreds of morning exercisers have told me that the gentle exertion, early, allowed the time and the mental energy to organize their day better than any other activity. Others said that the after-work "workout" relieved stress, tied up the mental loose ends from the office, and allowed for a transition to being at home. You will get as much (probably more) work done each day if you walk regularly. It is up to you to take charge so that you will inject walking—and energy—into your day.

I don't have the energy to walk today

This is one of the easier ones to solve. Most of the exercisers who've consulted me about this excuse had not been eating enough times a day. I don't mean eating more food. In most cases, the quantity of food is reduced. By eating about every 2-3 hours, most feel more energized, more of the time. Even if you aren't eating well during the day, you can overcome low blood sugar by having a "booster" snack about an hour before a walk. Caffeine helps (as long as you don't have caffeine sensitivities). My dynamic food duo is an energy bar and a cup of coffee. Just carry some food with you and energize yourself before you exercise. Again, you are taking charge.

I don't have my walking shoes and clothes with me

Take an old bag (backpack, etc.) and load it with a pair of walking shoes, a top for both winter and summer, shorts and warm-up pants, towel, deodorant, and anything else you would need for a walk and clean up.

Put the bag next to the front door, or in the trunk of your car, etc. Then, the next time you are waiting to pick up your child from soccer, etc, you can do a quick change in the restroom and make some loops around the field.

I'd rather be sitting on a couch eating candy

Ok, now it's time for your "test." What is your response to this type of message?

AND IF I DON'T DON'T ENJOY MY WALKING?

Are you tired when your start your walk, or a short distance into the walk?

This is often due to low blood sugar. Eat an energy bar and a cup of coffee (or beverage of your choice) about an hour before your walk.

Are you doing your walk in the same place, day after day?

If you are stuck walking in the same place, break out! Go to a scenic or interesting area at least once a week. Some folks are more motivated walking in the city, while others can't wait to enjoy a walk on trails. Whatever area motivates you to walk, go there.

Are you exercising at a fairly hard level, more than 3 days a week?

If you are tired or simply unmotivated, you may be hitting a temporary "burnout wall." Drop back to an every-other-day exercise routine until you feel the motivation come back. Most walkers in this position find that they respond better by only doing 10 minute sessions at first. After a week or two, 10 minutes is not enough.

Are you walking with a group?

The right group will keep you motivated. As you walk, you'll share stories, jokes...your life. There is something very gutteral about walking together that encourages you to be yourself and share with others. You don't want to miss the fun of the group.

Are you walking the same distance each day?

If so, vary the distance. Have one long one a week, one short one and one of medium distance. Variety is the spice of walking.

Do you walk at the same pace every day?

You'll tend to get into a boring rut if every day is the same. On your long day, go very slow. On your short day, walk faster in a few one minute segments than you normally walk (don't sprint, just go faster than normal). Look at the cadence drill mentioned in this book. Not only will this drill help you walk more easily and faster—the 20 second cadence counts will break up a walk and give you a purpose.

Do you have a goal?

Look at a schedule of running/walking events in your area and select one that you want to finish. If you have done this before you can also target a time goal. As you write the race date on the calendar, you'll find more purpose to every walk.

Have you just finished a long term goal?

When you have trained for a challenging event over several months, it's normal to have a letdown. You can avoid this by selecting a series of motivational walks (social, scenic, festival races) for the 2 months after your goal has been completed. Write them down on your calendar or in your training journal at least a month before your first goal. This creates mental motivation that bridges from one event to the next.

Are you writing down your walks in a training journal?

It's motivational to write down mileage, day after day. Often, after looking back over your log entries you can find a series of reasons why you are not motivated: did too much during a month, walked too fast, etc. Once you get into the habit of "journaling" you'll be energized by noting your mileage success each day—and motivated to avoid writing a zero.

Are you giving yourself rewards, every week or two?

A smoothie after a long walk, a pancake breakfast after walking with your group are two examples of food rewards. Our psyche responds positively to a wide range of reinforcements: social, clothing, equipment, emotional, and spiritual. Here are some examples of reinforcements you can say to yourself...to energize the spirit:

After a tough one—"I had to dig down deep today, but overcame adversity. I feel good!"

After a great relaxing walk—"There's no better way to clear the stress than a walk like this"

After your longest walk for the month—"I can't believe that I went so far!"

After finishing a walk, when you didn't think you would—"I feel so empowered I can do anything"

After a walk that was slower than you wanted—"I am miles ahead of those on the couch"

DEALING WITH THE WEATHER

*"Neither rain, nor ice, nor heat, nor gloom,
nor night shall keep us from our walk"*

Sometimes, on those snowy, rainy, brutally cold days, I yearn for the early days of exercise when I always used weather as an excuse for staying warm and cozy inside. Today, however, there are garments for each of the above, head to toe. Yes, technology has taken away most of our excuses for not exercising. But I've also found that lazy exercisers can be very creative. Every year I hear a few new excuses from this group who rise to the occasion with cleverness. In reality, even if you don't have the clothing for hot or cold weather, you can walk indoors—on treadmills, in malls or stadiums, or at a gym.

A few years ago, I visited Fairbanks, Alaska. I had to ask the members of the local running club what was the lowest temperature that anyone had endured. The "winner" had run a 10K in minus 66 (not wind-chill, this was the real thing: bulb temperature). He said it really didn't feel that cold. Sure!

The fact is that clothing designers have responded to the needs of exercisers during extreme weather conditions, making it possible to go outside, fairly comfortably, in sub zero conditions. I will admit, however, that if it is minus 66, I can't exercise because I have to rearrange my shoes next to a warm fire.

Exercising in hot weather

After decades of running in hot weather areas, mostly in Florida and Georgia, with some time spent in Hawaii and the Philippines, I haven't seen much in clothing that lowers body temperature. Clothing can minimize the temperature rise, while helping you feel cooler, and a bit more comfortable. But there are a number of other "tricks" you can play which will lower your temperature and keep you exercising.

When you exercise strenuously in high heat (above 70°F), or moderate heat (above 60°F) with high humidity (above 50%) you raise core body temperature. Most beginning exercisers will see their internal temperature rise above 55°F. This triggers a release of blood into the capillaries of your skin to help cool you down. But this diversion reduces the blood supply available to your exercising muscles, meaning that you will have less oxygen delivered to the power source that moves you forward—and less blood available to move out the waste products from these work sites.

The Bad News

In warm weather you are going to feel worse and should walk slower. If you build up the heat too quickly, stay out too long, or go too fast—for you—the result could be heat disease. Make sure that you read the section on this health problem at the end of this chapter.

The good news

You can adapt to these conditions to some extent, as you learn the best time of the day to exercise, clothing, and other tricks to keep you cool. There are some other good options below, so read on.

Walking through the summer heat

1. Walk before the sun gets above the horizon. Get up early during warm weather and you will avoid most of the dramatic stress from the sun. This is particularly a problem in humid areas. Early morning is usually the coolest time of the day, also. Without having to deal with the sun, most walkers can gradually adapt to heat. At the very least, your walks will be more enjoyable.

2. If you must walk when the sun is up, pick a shady course. Shade provides a significant relief in areas of low humidity, and some relief in humid environments.

3. Evening and night walking is usually cooler in areas with low humidity. In humid environments there may not be much relief.

Note: Be sure to take care of safety issues.

4. Have an indoor facility available. With treadmills, you can exercise in air conditioning. If a treadmill bores you, alternate segments of 5-10 minutes—one segment outdoors, and the next indoors.

5. Don't wear a hat! You lose most of your body heat through the top of your head. Covering the head will cause a quicker internal build-up of heat.

6. Wear light clothing, but not cotton. Many of the new, technical fibers (Polypro, Coolmax, Drifit, etc.) will move moisture away from your skin, producing a cooling effect. Cotton soaks up the sweat, making the garment heavier without as much of a cooling effect.

7. Pour water over your head. Evaporation not only helps the cooling process—it makes you feel cooler. If you can bring along ice water with you, you will feel a lot cooler as you squirt some regularly over the top of your head. Another trick is to carry a spray bottle and spray mist regularly.

8. Do your walk in installments. It is fine, on a hot day, to put in your 30 minutes by doing 10 in the morning, 10 at noon and 10 at night. The long one, however, should be done at one time.

9. Take a pool break, or a shower chill-down. During a walk, it really helps to take a 2-4 minute dip in a pool or a shower. Some walkers in hot areas walk loops around their neighborhood and let the hose run over the head each lap. The pool is especially helpful in soaking out excess body temperature. I have covered 5 miles in 97F degree temperatures at our Florida retreat area, breaking the workout into a series of 12-19 minute segments with a 2-3 minute "soak break." It is amazing how the pool soak can leave you refreshed for the next 10 minutes or so.

10. Sun screen—ask an expert. Some products produce a coating on the skin, slowing down the perspiration and causing an increase in body temperature build-up. If you are only in the sun for 10-30 minutes at a time, you may not need to put on sunscreen for cancer protection. Consult with a dermatologist for your specific needs—or find a product that doesn't block the pores.

11. Drink 6-8 oz of a sports drink like Accelerade or water at least every 2 hours, or when thirsty, throughout the day during hot weather.

12. Look at the clothing thermometer at the end of this section. Wear loose fitting garments that have some texture in the fabric. Texture will limit or prevent the perspiration from causing clinging and sticking to the skin.

13. If your only option is going outside on a very hot day, you have my permission to re-arrange your running shoes—preferably in an air-conditioned environment.

Heat disease alert!

While it is unlikely that you will push yourself into heat disease, the longer you are exercising in hot (and/or humid) conditions, the more you increase the likelihood of this dangerous medical situation. That's why I recommend breaking up your exercise into short segments when it's hot and you are forced to do all of the exertion outdoors. Be sensitive to your reactions to the heat, and those of the exercisers around you. When one of the symptoms is present, this is normally not a major problem unless there is significant distress. But when several are experienced, take action because heat disease can lead to death. It's always better to be conservative: stop the workout and cool off.

Symptoms:

- Intense heat build-up in the head
- General overheating of the body
- Significant headache
- Significant nausea
- General confusion and loss of concentration
- Loss of muscle control
- Excessive sweating and then cessation of sweating
- Clammy skin
- Excessively rapid breathing
- Muscle cramps
- Feeling faint

Risk factors:

- Viral or bacterial infection
- Taking medication—especially cold medicines, diuretics, medicines for diarrhea, antihistamines, atropine, scopolamine, tranquilizers
- Dehydration (especially due to alcohol)
- Severe sunburn

- Overweight
- Smoking
- Lack of heat training
- Exercising more than one is used to
- Occurrence of heat disease in the past
- Several nights of extreme sleep deprivation
- Certain medical conditions including high cholesterol, high blood pressure, extreme stress, asthma, diabetes, epilepsy, drug use (including alcohol), cardiovascular disease, smoking, or a general lack of fitness

Take action! Call 911

Use your best judgement, but in most cases anyone who exhibits two or more of the symptoms should get into a cool environment, and receive medical attention immediately. An extremely effective cool off method is to soak towels, sheets or clothing in cool or cold weather, and wrap them around the individual. If ice is available, sprinkle some ice over the wet cloth.

Heat adaptation workout

If you regularly force yourself to deal with body heat build-up, your body will adapt to it. As with all training components, it is important to do this regularly. You should be sweating to some extent at the end of the workout, although the amount and the duration of perspiration is an individual issue. If the heat is causing unusual stress, cut back the amount.

Important Note: Read the section on heat disease and stop this workout if you sense that you are even beginning to become nauseous, lose concentration or mental awareness of your condition, etc.

- Do this on a short walk day once a week
- Do the walk-shuffle ratio you usually use, going at a comfortable pace
- Warm up with a 5 minute easy walk and take a 5 minute slow walk warm down
- Temperature should be between 75°F and 85°F (22-27°C) for best results
- Stop at the first sign of nausea or significant heat stress
- When less than 70°F (19°C), you can put on additional layers of clothing to simulate a higher temperature.
- First session, walk for only 3-4 minutes in the heat
- Each successive session, add 2-3 minutes

Tip: Maintaining heat tolerance during the winter

During the cold weather months, you can maintain much of your summer heat conditioning with this workout. Put on additional layers of clothing so that you sweat within 3-4 minutes of your walk. Continue to walk for a total of 5-12 minutes at an easy pace. Don't push yourself into heat stress that could cause heat disease.

What about dealing with cold weather?

While most of my exercise sessions have been in temperatures above 60°F (14°C), I've also run in minus 30°(C & F are about equal). I prepared for this excursion by donning as many layers as I had in my suitcase. When I met my guide for this outing he quickly evaluated my clothing and found me lacking. After another two layers I was ready to go.

The specific type of garments, especially the one next to your skin, is an individual issue. I'm not going to get into the specifics here because the technology changes quickly. In general, you want your first layer to be comfortable and not too thick. There are a number of fabrics today, mostly man-made, that hold a comfortable amount of body heat close to the skin to keep you warm, but don't let you overheat. Most of these same fibers allow for moisture, such as perspiration and rain, to be moved away from the skin even as you walk. Not only does this add to your comfort in winter, but almost eliminates a chill due to having wet skin in a cold wind.

Don't underestimate the chill of winter – some tips

1. Expand your lunch hour if you want to walk outdoors. Mid-day is usually the warmest time period, so you will probably have to plan to arrive at work early (pay bills, run errands, etc.). The mid-day sun can make your outdoor walking much more comfortable—even when it is very cold.

2. If early morning is the only time you can walk, bundle up. The "clothing thermometer" at the end of this section will help you to dress for the temperature and not over-dress. Individualize as necessary.

3. Walk into the wind at the start, particularly when you are walking in one direction and turning around. If you walk with the wind at your back for the first half, you'll tend to sweat. When you then turn into a cold wind, you'll chill down dramatically.

4. Having a health club will give you an indoor venue, and other exercise opportunity. Treadmills allow you to walk without the wind chill. I have worked with many exercisers who hate treadmills, but also hate cold weather. Their compromise is to alternate segments of 7-15 minutes—one segment outdoors, and the next

indoors. Count the transition as a shuffle break. Health clubs expand your exercise horizons offering a variety of alternative exercise.

5. One of your exercise days could be a Triathlon—your choice of three exercises. You can do exercises out of your home, or at a health club.

6. Seek out a large indoor facility near your office or home. In Houston, runners use the tunnels below city streets. Many northern cities offer skyways and allow runners and walkers to use them when traffic allows it. Domes, malls and civic centers often allow winter walkers at certain times.

7. Wear a hat! You lose most of your body heat through the top of your head. Covering the head will help you retain body heat and stay warm.

8. Cover your extremities from the wind chill you produce when you walk in the cold! Protect ears, hands, nose and generally the front of the face. Make sure that you protect the feet with socks that are thick enough. And men, wear an extra pair of underwear.

8. As suggested in warm weather, do your daily walking "quota" in installments. It is fine, on a really cold day, to put in your 30 minutes by doing 10 in the morning, 10 at noon and 10 at night.

9. Take a "warm up" break. Before you head out into the cold, walk in place, indoors—or do other exercise that raises body temperature. During a walk, when you get really cold outside, it really helps to take a 2-4 minute walk indoors. Some walkers schedule their shuffle breaks to coincide with buildings that allow public walking.

10. Vaseline—be sure to protect yourself wherever there is exposed skin on very cold days. One area, for example, is the skin around the eyes, not protected by a ski mask, etc.

11. When you are exercising during the winter, indoor or outdoor, you will be losing almost as much in sweat as in the warm months. You should still drink at least 4-6 oz of a sports drink like Accelerade or water at least every 2 hours, or when thirsty, throughout the day.

12. Another reminder: Look at the clothing thermometer at the end of this section and customize it for your situation.

Clothing thermometer

After years of working with people in various climates, here are my recommendations for the appropriate clothing based upon the temperature. As always, however, wear what works best for you. The general rule is to choose your garments by function first. And remember that the most important layer for comfort is the one next to your skin. Garments made out of fabric labeled Polypro, Coolmax, Drifit, etc., hold body heat close to you in winter, while releasing extra heat. In summer and winter, the tech fabrics move moisture away from the skin—cooling you in hot weather, and helping to avoid a chill in the winter.

Temperature	What to wear
14°C or 60°F and above	Tank top or singlet, and shorts
9 to13°C or 50 to 59°F	T-shirt and shorts
5 to 8°C or 40 to 49°F	Long sleeve lightweight shirt, shorts or tights (or nylon long pants),mittens and gloves
0 to 4°C or 30 to 39°F	Long sleeve medium weight shirt, and another T-shirt, tights and shorts, socks or mittens or gloves and a hat over the ears
-4 to –1°C or 20-29°F	Medium weight long sleeve shirt, another T-shirt, tights and shorts, sockssocks, mittens or gloves, and a hat over the ears
-8 to –3°C or 10-19°F	Medium weight long sleeve shirt, and medium/heavy weight shirt, tights and shorts, nylon wind suit, top and pants, socks, thick mittens and a hat over the ears
-12 to –7°C or 0-9°F	Two medium or heavyweight long sleeve tops, thick tights, thick underwear (especially for men), medium to heavy warm up, gloves and thick mittens, ski mask, a hat over the ears, and Vaseline covering any exposed skin.

-18 to –11 °C or –15 °F	Two heavyweight long sleeve tops, thick tights, thick underwear (and supporter for men), thick warm up (top and pants) mittens over gloves, thick ski mask and a hat over ears, Vaseline covering any exposed skin, thicker socks on your feet and other foot protection, as needed.
Minus 20° both C & F	Add layers as needed

What not to wear

1. A heavy coat in winter. If the layer is too thick, you'll heat up, sweat excessively, and cool too much when you take it off.

2. No shirt for men in summer. Fabric that holds some of the moisture will give you more of a cooling effect as you walk.

3. Too much sun screen—it can interfere with sweating

4. Socks that are too thick in summer. Your feet swell and the pressure from the socks can increase the chance of a black toenail and blisters.

5. Lime green shirt with bright pink polka dots (unless you have a lot of confidence).

CRAMPS, DOGS, AND OTHER PROBLEMS

- Coming back after a layoff from walking
- It hurts!
- No energy…
- Side Pain
- I feel great one day—but the next day…
- No motivation
- Cramps in my leg muscles
- Upset stomach or diarrhea
- Headache
- Should I walk when I have a cold?
- Street safety
- Dogs
- Heart disease and walking

What is the best way to start back after some time off?

The longer you've been away from walking, the more conservative you should be when you start back. I want to warn you now that you will reach a point when you feel totally back in shape—but you are not. Stay with the plan below for your return and when in doubt, be more conservative. Remember that you are in this for the long run…or walk!

Less than 2 weeks off You will feel like you are starting over again, but should come back quickly. Look back at the schedules in the early chapters of this book. Let's say you were at week #20, but had to take 10 days off. Start back at week #2 for the first week. If all is well, skip to week # 4 for the second week. If that works well, gradually transition back to the schedule you were using before you had your layoff, over the next 2-3 weeks.

14 days to 29 days off You will also feel like you are starting over again, and it will take longer to get it all back: Within about 5-6 weeks you should be back to normal. Use the schedule of your choice (from week #1) for two weeks. If there are no aches, pains or lingering fatigue, then use the schedule but skip every other week. After the 5th week, transition back into what you were doing before the layoff.

One month or more off If you have not walked for a month or more, start over again, like a beginner. Use one of the three schedules in this book, following it exactly (from week #1) for the first few weeks. After 2-3 weeks, the safest plan is to continue with the schedule. But if you're having no aches and pains, and no lingering fatigue, you could increase more rapidly by skipping one week out of three. After 2 months of no problems, you could skip every other week, if everything is still feeling great.

Ouch! It hurts!

Is it just a passing ache, or a real injury?

Most of the aches and pains you feel when walking will go away within a minute or two. If the pain comes on, just walk for an additional 2 minutes, shuffle for 2 minutes, and walk another 2 minutes using a very short stride—then sit down and massage the hurt area, if you can. If the pain comes back after doing this 4 or 5 times, stop the workout and shuffle back to your house or car. If the pain goes away when you shuffle, just shuffle for the rest of the walk.

It's an injury if...

There's inflammation—swelling in the area
There's loss of function—the foot, knee, etc. doesn't work correctly
There's pain—it hurts and keeps hurting or gets worse

Treatment suggestions

1. See a doctor who has treated runners and walkers very successfully and wants to get you back on the road or trail.

2. Take at least 2-5 days off from any activity that could irritate it to get the healing started, more if needed.

3. If the area is next to the skin (tendon, foot, etc), rub a chunk of ice on the area(s)—constantly rubbing for 15 min until the area gets numb. Continue to do this for a week after you feel no symptoms. Ice bags and gel ice do no good at all in most cases (ankle sprains and other trauma injuries may benefit from packing ice around the injury site. Ask your doctor).

4. If the problem is inside a joint or muscle, call your doctor and ask if you can use prescription strength anti-inflammatory medication. Don't take any medication without a doctor's advice—and follow that advice.

5. If you have a muscle injury, see a veteran sports massage therapist. Try to find one who has a lot of successful experience treating the area where you are injured. The magic fingers and hands can often work wonders.

This is advice from one walker to another. For more info on injuries, treatment, etc. see the "injury free" chapter in this book, and *Galloway's Book On Running, Second Edition*.

No fuel in the tank today

When you find yourself sluggish and not wanting to exercise, you can often turn it around and feel great. Occasionally, you will not be able to do this, because of an infection, lingering fatigue, or other physical problems. But here's a list of things that can give you energy. If these actions don't help you get moving down the road, then read the nutrition sections—particularly the blood sugar chapter in this book—or in *Galloway's Book On Running, Second Edition*.

1. Eat an energy bar, with water or caffeinated beverage, about an hour before the walk.

2. Instead of #1, half an hour before exercising, drink 100-200 calories of a sports drink that has a mix of 80% simple carbohydrate and 20% protein. The product Accelerade has this already put together.

3. Just walk for 5 minutes away from your house, office, etc., and the energy often kicks in. Forward movement gets the attitude moving too.

4. One of the prime reasons for no energy, is that you didn't re-load within 30 minutes after your last exercise session: 200-300 calories of a mix that is 80% simple carbohydrate and 20% protein (Endurox R4 is the product that has this formulated).

5. Low carbohydrate diets will result in low energy to get you motivated before a workout, and often no energy to finish the workout.

6. In most cases it is fine to keep going even if you aren't energetic. But if you sense an infection, see a doctor. If the low energy stays around for several days, see a nutritionist that knows about the special needs of exercisers and/or get some blood work done. This may be due to inadequate iron, B vitamins, energy stores, etc.

Note:
If you have any problems with caffeine, don't consume any products containing it. As always, if you sense any health problem, see a doctor.

A stitch in the side

This is very common, and usually has a simple fix. Normally it is not anything to worry about...it just hurts. This condition is due to 1) the lack of deep breathing, and 2) going a little too fast from the beginning of the walk. You can correct #2 easily by walking more slowly at the beginning, and slowing down your walking pace.

Deep breathing from the beginning of a walk can prevent side pain. This way of inhaling air is performed by diverting the air you breathe into your lower lungs. Also called "belly breathing," this is how we breathe when asleep, and it provides maximum opportunity for oxygen absorption. If you don't use this deep breathing technique when you walk, and you are not getting the oxygen you need, the side pain will tell you. By slowing down, walking, and breathing deeply for a while, the pain may go away. But sometimes it does not. Most exercisers just continue to walk with the side pain. After about 50 years of exercising, and helping others, I've not seen any lasting negative effect from those who walk with a side pain.

Tip: Some walkers have found that side pain goes away if they tightly grasp a rock in the hand that is on the side of the pain. Squeeze it for 15 seconds or so. Keep squeezing 3-5 times.

Note: Never breathe in and out rapidly. This can lead to hyperventilation, dizziness, and fainting.

You don't have to take in a maximum breath to perform this technique. Simply breathe a normal breath but send it to the lower lungs. You know that you have done this if your stomach goes up and down as you inhale and exhale. If your chest goes up and down, you are breathing shallowly.

But I felt great yesterday!

This is one of the great mysteries of the world, and if you can solve this problem, you could become a very wealthy person. There are a few common reasons for this, but there will always be "those days" when the body doesn't seem to work right, or the gravity seems heavier than normal—and you cannot find a reason.

1. Pushing through. In most cases, this is a one-day occurrence. Most walkers just put more shuffle breaks into the mix, and get through it. Before pushing, however, make sure that you don't have a medical reason why you feel bad.

2. Heat and/or Humidity will make you feel worse. You will often feel great when the temperature is below 60°F and miserable when 75°F or above

3. Low blood sugar can make any walk a bad one. You may feel good at the start and suddenly feel like you have no energy. Every step seems to take a major effort. Read the chapter in this book about this topic.

4. Low motivation. Use the rehearsal techniques in the "staying motivated" chapter to get you out the door on a bad day. These have helped numerous walkers turn their minds around—even in the middle of a walk.

5. Infection can leave you feeling lethargic, achy, and unable to walk at the same pace that was easy a few days earlier. Check the normal signs (fever, chills, swollen lymph glands, etc.) and at least call your doctor if you suspect something.

6. Medication and alcohol, even when taken the day before, can leave a hangover that dampens a workout.

7. A slower start can make the difference between a good day and a bad day. When your body is on the edge of fatigue or other stress, it only takes a few seconds too fast per mile, to push into discomfort or worse.

Muscle cramps

Sooner or later, almost anyone who walks, particularly in hot weather, experiences muscle cramps. These muscle contractions usually occur in the feet or the calf muscles and may come during a walk, or they may hit at random. Most commonly, they will occur at night, or when you are sitting around at your desk or watching TV in the afternoon or evening

Cramps vary in severity. Most are mild but some can grab so hard that they shut down the muscles and hurt when they seize up. Massage, and a short and gentle movement of the muscle can help to bring most of the cramps around. Odds are that stretching will make the cramp worse, or tear the muscle fibers.

Most cramps are due to overuse—doing more than in the recent past, or continuing to put yourself at your limit, especially in warm weather. Look at the pace and distance of your walks in your training journal to see if you have been going too far, or too fast, or both.

- Continuous walking at the same effort and pace increases the chance of cramping. Taking shuffle breaks more often can reduce or eliminate cramps. I've known many exercisers who used to cramp when they walked for 3-4 minutes and shuffled a minute, but stopped cramping with a ratio of walk 1-2 minutes and shuffle 1-2 minutes.
- During hot weather, a good electrolyte beverage can help to replace the salts your body loses sweating. A drink like Accelerade, for example, can help to top off these minerals when drinking 6-8 oz every 1-2 hours.
- On very long hikes, or walks, however, the continuous sweating, especially when drinking a lot of fluid, can push your sodium levels too low and produce muscle

cramping. If this happens regularly, a buffered salt tablet has helped greatly: Succeed.

- Many medications, especially those designed to lower cholesterol, have as one of their known side effects, muscle cramps. Walkers who use medications and cramp should ask their doctor if there are alternatives.

Note:
If you have high blood pressure, ask your doctor before taking any salt product.

Dealing with cramps:
1. Take a longer and more gentle warm-up
2. Shorten your walk segment
3. Slow down your shuffle, and shuffle more
4. Shorten your distance on a hot/humid day
5. Break your walk up into two segments
6. Look at any other exercise that could be causing the cramps
7. Take a buffered salt tablet at the beginning of your exercise

Upset stomach or diarrhea – you can blame it on stress

Sooner or later, virtually every walker has at least one episode with nausea or diarrhea (N/D). It comes from the build-up of total stress that you accumulate. Most commonly, it is the stress of walking on that day, due to the causes listed below. But stress is the result of many unique conditions within the individual. Your body triggers the (N/D) to get you to reduce the exercise, which will reduce the stress. Here are the common causes.

1. Walking too fast or too far is the most common cause. Walkers are confused about this, because the pace doesn't feel too fast in the beginning. Each person has a level of fatigue that triggers these conditions. Slowing down and taking more shuffle breaks will help you manage the problem.

2. Eating too much or too soon before the walk. Your system has to work hard when walking with a full stomach. Trying to digest and walk at the same time raises stress and results in nausea, etc. Having food in your stomach, in the process of being digested, is an extra stress and a likely target for elimination.

3. Eating a high fat or high protein diet. Even one meal that has over 50% of the calories in fat or protein can lead to N/D hours later.

4. Eating too much the afternoon or evening, the day before. A big evening meal will still be in the gut the next morning, being digested. When you bounce up and down on a walk, which you will, you add stress to the system and can result in (N/D).

5. Heat and humidity are a major cause of these problems. Some people don't adapt to heat well and experience N/D with minimal build-up of temperature or humidity. But in hot conditions, everyone has a core body temperature increase that will result in significant stress to the system—often causing nausea, and sometimes diarrhea. By slowing down, taking more shuffle breaks, and pouring water over your head, you can manage this better.

6. Drinking too much water before a walk. If you have too much water in your stomach, and you are bouncing around, you put stress on the digestive system. Reduce your intake to the bare minimum. Most walkers don't need to drink any fluid before a walk that is 60 minutes or less.

7. Drinking too much of a sugar/electrolyte drink. Water is the easiest substance for the body to process. The addition of sugar and/or electrolyte minerals, as in a sports drink, makes the substance harder to digest. During a walk (especially on a hot day) I suggest only water. Cold water is best.

8. Drinking too much fluid too soon after a walk. Even if you are very thirsty, don't gulp down large quantities of any fluid. Try to drink no more than 6-8 oz, every 20 minutes or so. If you are particularly prone to this N/D, just take 2-4 sips, every 5 minutes or so. When the body is very stressed and tired, it's not a good idea to consume a sugar drink. The extra stress of digesting the sugar can lead to problems.
9. Don't let walking be stressful to you. Some walkers get too obsessed about getting their walk in or walking at a specific pace. This adds stress to your life. Relax and let your walk erase some of the other tensions in your life.

Headache

There are several reasons why exercisers get headaches during or after exercise. While uncommon, they happen to the average walker a few times a year, and are usually due to causes other than exercise. The little bit of dehydration stress that walking puts on the body can trigger a headache on a tough day—even considering the relaxation that comes from the walk. Usually, a dose of an over-the-counter headache medication takes care of the problem. As always, consult with your doctor about use of medication. Here are the causes/solutions.

Dehydration—if you walk in the morning, make sure that you hydrate well the day before. Avoid alcohol the night before if you're a morning walker who has headaches. Also watch the salt in your dinner meal the night before. A good sports drink like accelerade, taken throughout, the day before, will help to keep your fluid levels and your electrolytes "topped off." If you exercise in the afternoon, follow the same advice leading up to your walk.

Medications can often produce dehydration—There are some medications that make exercisers more prone to headaches. Check with your doctor.

Too hot for you—walk at a cooler time of the day (usually in the morning before the sun gets above the horizon). On a hot day, pour water over your head.

Walking a little too fast—start all walks more slowly, shuffle more during the first half

Walking further than you have gone in the recent past—monitor your mileage and don't increase more than about 15% further than you have walked on any single session in the past week.

Low blood sugar level—be sure that you boost your BSL with a snack, about 30-60 min before you walk. If you are used to having it, caffeine in a beverage can sometimes help this situation also.

If prone to migranes—generally avoid caffeine, and try your best to avoid dehydration. Talk to your doctor about other possibilities.

Watch your neck and lower back—if you have a slight forward lean as you walk, you can put pressure on the spine—particularly in the neck and lower back. Read the form chapter in this book and walk upright.

Is it OK to walk when I have a cold?

There are so many individual health issues with a cold that you must talk with a doctor before you exercise when you have an infection.

Lung infection—don't exercise! A virus in the lungs can move into the heart and kill you. Lung infections are usually indicated by coughing. Call your doctor for direction.

Common cold? There are many infections that initially seem to be a normal cold but are not. At least call your doctor's office to get clearance before exercise. Be sure to explain how much you are walking, and what, if any, medication you are taking.

*Throat infection and above—*most walkers will be given the OK, but check with the doctor.

Be street-smart about street safety

Each year several walkers are hit by cars. Most of these accidents are preventable. Here are the primary reasons and what you can do about them.

1. **The driver is intoxicated or preoccupied by cell phone, etc**
    Always be on guard—even when walking on the sidewalk or pedestrian trail. Many of the fatal crashes occurred when the driver lost control of the car, and came up from behind, on the wrong side of the road. I know it is wonderful to be on "cruise control" in your right brain, but you can avoid a life-threatening situation if you will just keep looking around, and anticipate.

2. **The walker dashes across an intersection against the traffic light**
    When walking with another person, don't follow blindly across an intersection. Those who quickly sprint across the street without looking are often surprised by cars coming from unexpected directions. The best rule

is the one that you heard as a child: When you get to an intersection, stop, see what the traffic situation is. Look both ways, and look both ways again (and again) before crossing. Have an option to bail out of the crossing if a car surprises you from any direction.

3. **Sometimes, walkers wander out into the street as they talk**

One of the very positive aspects of walking (social time) becomes a negative one in this case. Yes, chat and enjoy time with your friends. But every walker in a group needs to be responsible for his or her own safety, footing, etc. The biggest mistake I see is that the walkers at the back of a group assume that they don't have to be concerned about traffic at all—because the ones ahead are looking out for them. This lack of concern is a very risky situation.

- In general, be ready to save yourself from a variety of traffic problems by following the rules below and any others that apply to specific situations. Even though the rules below seem obvious, many accidents occur each year because pedestrians ignore them.
- Be constantly aware of vehicular traffic, at all times, from every possible direction.
- Assume that all drivers are drunk or crazy or both. When you see a strange movement by a car, be ready to get out of the way.
- Mentally practice running for safety. Get into the practice of thinking ahead at all times, with a plan for each current stretch of road.
- Walk as far off the road as you can. If possible use on a sidewalk or pedestrian trail instead of the street.
- Walk facing traffic. A high percentage of traffic deaths come from those who go with the flow of traffic (even

though they are off the road), and do not see the threat from behind.

- Wear reflective gear at night. I've heard the accounts and this apparel has saved lives.
- Take control over your safety—you are the only one on the road who will usually save yourself.

Dogs: Not necessarily a walker's best friend

When you enter a dog's territory, you may be in for a confrontation. Here are my suggestions for dealing with your "dog days":

1. There are several good devices that will help deter dogs: an old fashioned stick, rocks, some electronic signal devices, pepper spray. If you are in a new area, or an area of known dogs, I recommend that you have one of these at all times.

2. At the first sign of a dog ahead, or barking, try to figure out where the dog is located, whether the dog is a real threat, and what territory the dog is guarding.

3. The best option is to walk a different route.

4. If you really want or need to walk past the dog, pick up a rock if you don't have another anti-dog device.

5. Watch the tail. If the tail does not wag, beware.

6. As you approach the dog it is natural for the dog to bark and head toward you. Raise your rock as if you will throw it at the dog. In my experience, the dog withdraws about 90% of the time. You may need to do this several times before getting through the dog's territory. Keep your arms up.

7. In a few cases you will need to throw the rock, and sometimes another if the dog keeps coming.

8. In less that 1% of the hundreds of dog confrontations I've had, there is something wrong with the dog, and it continues to move toward you. Usually the hair will be

up on the dog's back, and the tail is not wagging. Try to find a barrier to get behind, yell loudly in hopes that the owner or someone will help you. If a car comes by, try to flag down the driver, and either stay behind the car as you get out of the dog's territory, or get in the car for protection if that is appropriate.

9. Develop your own voice. Some use a deep commanding voice, some use a high pitched voice. Whichever you use, exude confidence and command.

TROUBLE SHOOTING ACHES AND PAINS

At the first sign of soreness or irritation in these areas, read the injury chapter. It is always better to take 2-3 days off from walking, and then start back making some form adjustments. In most of these areas, I've found that stretching aggravates the problem. For more information, see *Galloway's Book On Running, Second Edition*—which has an expanded injury section.

Front of Shin (lower leg): Soreness or pain in the anterior tibial area

Note: Even after you make the corrections, shin problems often take several weeks to heal. As long as the shin problem is not a stress fracture, easy walking can often allow it to heal as quickly (or more quickly) than complete layoff. In general, most walkers can walk when they have shin splints—they just need to stay below the threshold of further irritation.

Causes:
1. Increasing too rapidly—just walk for 1-2 weeks at shorter distances with a short stride, gently.
2. Walking too fast, even on one day—when in doubt, walk slower on every walk.
3. Walking with a stride that is too long—shorten stride and use more of a "shuffle."

Inside of Shin: Soreness or pain in the posterior tibial area

Causes
1. Same three causes as in anterior tibial shin splints, above.

2. More common with walkers who over-pronate. This means that they tend to roll to the inside of the forefoot as they push off.

3. Shoes may be too soft, allowing a floppy/pronated foot to roll inward more than usual.

Corrections:

1. Reduce stride length.
2. Put more shuffling into your walk from the beginning.
3. If you are an over-pronator on the forward part of your feet, get a stable, motion control shoe.
4. Ask your foot doctor if there is a foot device that can help you.

Shoulder and neck muscles tired and tight

Primary cause:

leaning too far forward as you walk.

Other causes:

1. Holding arms too far away from the body.
2. Swinging arms and shoulders too much.

Corrections:

1. Use the "puppet on a string" image (detailed in the form chapter) about every 4-5 minutes during all walks—particularly the longer ones. This is noted above in the section on posture. (check indents)
2. Watch how you are holding your arms. Try to keep the arms close to the body.
3. Minimize the swing of your arms. Keep the hands close to the body, lightly touching your shirt or the outside of your shorts as your arms swing.

Lower Back: Tight, sore, or painful after a walk

Causes
1. Leaning too far forward.
2. Having a stride length that is too long for you.

Corrections:
1. Use the "puppet on a string image several times on all walks—particularly the longer ones. This is noted in the chapter on form, in the section on posture.
2. Ask a physical therapist whether some strengthening exercise can help
3. When in doubt, shorten your stride length.
4. For more information, see *Galloway's Book On Running, Second Edition*.

Knee pain at the end of a walk

Causes:
1. Stride length could be too long.
2. Doing too much, too soon.
3. Not inserting enough shuffle breaks, regularly, from the beginning.
4. When the main walking muscles get tired, you will tend to wobble from side to side.

Corrections;
1. Shorten stride.
2. Stay closer to the ground, using more of a shuffle.
3. Monitor your mileage in a log book, and hold your increase to less than 10% a week.
4. Use more shuffle breaks during your walk.
5. Start at a slower pace.

Behind the knee: pain, tightness, or continued soreness or weakness

Causes:
1. Stretching.
2. Over striding—particularly at the end of the walk.

Corrections:
1. Don't stretch.
2. Keep your stride length under control.
3. Keep feet low to the ground.
4. As the leg swings behind you, don't let your leg be stiff and locked into position as you absorb body weight.

Hamstrings: tightness, soreness, or pain

Causes:
1. Stretching.
2. Stride length too long.
3. Lifting the foot too high behind, as your leg swings back.

Corrections:
1. Don't stretch.
2. Maintain a short stride, keeping the hamstring relaxed—especially at the end of the walk.
3. Take more shuffling early in the walk, possibly throughout.
4. As the leg swings behind you, don't let your leg be stiff and locked into position as you absorb body weight.
5. Deep tissue massage can sometimes help with this muscle group.

Quadriceps (front of the thigh): sore, tired, painful

Causes:

1. Lifting your knee too high—especially when tired.
2. Using the quads to slow down going downhill—because you were walking too fast or had a stride that was too long.

Corrections:

1. Maintain little or no knee lift—especially at the end of your walk.
2. Walk with a shuffle.
3. Let your stride get very short at the top of hills, and when tired—don't lengthen it.
4. If you are walking too fast going down hills, keep shortening stride until you slow down, and/or take more shuffle breaks on the downhill.

Sore feet or lower legs

Causes:

1. Too much bounce when you push off.
2. Pushing off too hard.
3. Shoes don't fit correctly or are too worn out.
4. Insole of shoe is worn out.

Corrections:

1. Keep feet low to the ground.
2. Maintain a light touch of the feet.
3. Get a shoe check to see if your shoes are too worn.
4. You may need only a new insole.

EXERCISE AFTER 40, 50, 60, 70

I can't tell you how many time I hear people tell me by the dozens how they wish they had started exercising earlier so they could do some kind of endurance activity. They are convinced it is too late for them. Within a few minutes, these folks wish they hadn't said what they said—to me. I tell them that I work with hundreds of people every year who are in their 40s, 50s, 60s, 70s and even 80s who are taking their first steps. Most of these folks become long distance walkers—some runners within 6 months. Many of them finish marathons—yes, even the 80-year-olds—within a year.

The principles of training which are described in this book apply to everyone—at any age. If you add a little stress followed by rest for recovery, your body rebuilds stronger.

The psychological rewards are the same at any age. Endorphins make your muscles feel better. You have a better attitude all day after a walk. Each walk brings a special relaxation not bestowed by other activities.

Elliott Galloway

As my father got more obese in his 40s, and more out of shape, he gave me every excuse one can imagine why he couldn't exercise. By his 50th birthday, even I had pretty much given up on trying to get him to exert himself. His "reality check" was a high school reunion.

Out of 25 guys who had been on his football team, only 12 were alive at age 52. As he drove home, the advice of his doctor and others came back to him. He realized that he could be the next to depart this world, at a time that he was just getting into his life's work—the founding of an innovative school.

Finally, he was motivated to exercise. Having been an all-state athlete, he knew that after a short warm up, he could zoom past the middle age people who were walking around the park. He was shocked to find that when he tried to run, for about the length of a football field, his legs gave out on him. He walked back. Every other day his mission was to make it to one more telephone pole before walking back. Within a year he was regularly making it around the golf course in front of his office, 3 miles. A year after that, he completed "The Peachtree Road Race 10K." After another 3 year's training, he completed a marathon. I'm most proud of the fact that in his mid 80s, my Dad is still walking over 20 miles a week.

Today I work with dozens of exercisers who consider themselves "over the hill." But even the 80+ year old beginners get caught up in the excitement of getting more fit. They cannot believe how much better they feel—every day. Honestly, these people are my heroes. I hope I can be like them when I grow up.

Recovery takes a little longer once you hit 40

Having run since I was 13, I've noticed subtle changes not usually noticeable during a 12-month period. It's only when I now look back over almost 5 decades of endurance exercise that I see the trends and the cruel facts.

1. Your recovery rate slows down each year past the age of 40.
2. At the same time, your mental focus usually increases so you can push yourself further into fatigue.
3. By the age of 55, there has been a significant slowdown from the age of 40.
4. By the age of 65, another significant slowdown has occurred—even from 55.

5. Training at a pace that is hard for you without making adjustments for getting older, will produce injuries, lingering fatigue or burnout.
6. It takes longer to warm up for each walk, each decade.
7. Any type of fast walking will increase the time needed for recovery.
8. Any significant increase in distance will increase the time needed for recovery.

So how many days should I walk every week?

I am not advocating that you try to exercise as many days as I do. After about 50 years of running, I've discovered many intuitive tricks, and haven't had a single over-use injury in over 25 years. Feel free to follow that part of my example.

Exercising every other day reduces the risk of aches, pains, burnout and fatigue. With an easy day between walks, you'll maintain conditioning through the decades. Even when walkers maintain the same weekly mileage, they reduce injury risk by walking fewer days per week.

Walking days per week based on your age

If you are experiencing more injuries, fatigue, or less enjoyment, walk fewer days

Below 35 years old	36-45 years old	46-55 years old	56-65 years old	66-75 years old	76 + years old
No more than 5 days	4 days	every other day	3 days	2 short/ 2longer	2short/ 1long

Just what is it you want to get out of your walking?

This is the most important question for anyone to answer—but especially for exercisers over 40. For me, the answer is simple—I want to be able to cover several miles almost every day, injury-free, for the rest of my life. That is why I slow down and walk often. My ego has been able to adjust to a slower pace, and I know that I feel better every day because I go slowly.

As I mentioned in the first chapter, you are the captain of your ship. If you want to keep increasing distance every month, or maintain a certain pace, or win your age group in the local walking races, it is your right to go for it. But have the phone numbers of your sports medicine doctors handy.

But for each goal, you must take responsibility for the consequences. In other words, if you get injured by trying to stay up with another person or group that is faster than you, realize that you put this on yourself.

You have lots of choices as to what you want to see as your final fitness product, each day and each year. Think carefully and structure accordingly.

A few mini-thoughts for you to consider...

One of the cruel hoaxes that the body plays on us is that even in our 60's we can get inspired and push ourselves beyond what we are ready to do—without feeling the warning signs during the exercise session. Unfortunately, the recovery time required after these power workouts is substantial, compared with the way it was 20-30 years ago.

* Making a "social walk" into a race. It is too easy to get led astray when we are feeling good—especially when

walking with a very fit friend, setting a faster pace than we are used to walking. Older walkers will often find that their walking stride may feel easy at the beginning, and sometimes at the end. But the next day, and the day after, it is a different story.

- Trying to walk no slower than a certain time produces great fatigue on warm days, hilly courses, etc. Mind games work against us as we get older. Your mind can remember when a certain pace was easy and will get you focused to stay on track for that goal. It is better to be flexible with distance, pace, course, and weather— and slow down under adversity. This can allow you to cover the same distance as you get older.

- Junk miles are easier walks on days that would be better spent as no-walk, recovery days. In almost every case it is better to take the day off when you are starting to feel the build-up of aches, pains, fatigue. You can then add the miles to other walking days that week.

- Starting walks too fast—usually with a stride that is too long—produces much greater fatigue. Your legs will feel so much better if you walk more gently than you could, during the first 2-3 miles

- Over-stretching tears muscle and tendon fibers and increases healing time for all walkers. This damage takes longer to repair as you get older. It doesn't take much of a stretch to be an over-stretch. Since I've not found stretching to be of benefit for almost all walkers I've worked with, I don't recommend it. If you like to stretch, be very careful.

- Pushing beyond your speed or endurance limit for a mile or more will greatly increase the time needed for recovery. Even younger walkers must pay for these violations. Older walkers pay by not having legs that are bouncy and resilient for a significant period after pushing too hard.

- Walking form violations produce more fatigue and muscle damage as we age
  - striding too long
  - pushing off too hard from the foot
  - kicking behind you too far

- Refusing to take shuffle breaks more often because it is too "wimpy." I'm proud to be a wimp who exercises about every single day—instead of being forced to be a couch sitter because of never taking a break.

SWITCHING ROLES - BEING A GOOD COACH

CHEATHAM HILL 26 MI
KOLB FARM 55 MI

One of the very best ways to consolidate the items you've learned from exercise is to help someone get started. Not only will you realize how much you have learned. You'll find that you see the "big picture" better as you explain the benefits of exercise to a novice.

But the best part of this experience is the inner satisfaction. You're not only helping someone, you're introducing him or her to an activity that can improve the quality of their life— for the rest of their life.

Buy them a good book—this book

Go over a chapter at a time, starting at the beginning. Highlight the key passages in the book for him or her. You don't have to do this on every chapter, but it really helps to get each novice headed in the right direction.

Keep it fun—especially during the first month

If your coachee is huffing and puffing, slow down and shuffle more from the beginning of every session. If there is continuing struggle, then stop for that day. There shouldn't be any huffing and puffing for several months, if then.

When you suspect even the possibility of low blood sugar, share an energy bar and coffee, tea, diet drink, etc. about 30-45 minutes before the start. Have a reward after each session—especially a snack to reload composed of 80% carbohydrate and 20% protein.

On some special occasions, however, it's OK to have a reward snack that may be a little more decadent than usual.

Provide a change of scenery—find interesting areas to walk

Convenient walking routes near work or home, are best for busy people, most of the time.

But once a week, an excursion to an interesting area can be very rewarding. It's great to have variety, and you should give your coachee some choice.

Take along a joke, a story, or a hot topic of conversation

This will break the ice, inject some humor, and help to make for a positive bonding experience. With beginners who are having a hard time getting into it, the little humorous items are often appreciated as much as the shoes and clothing.

Encourage without pushing too hard

One of the most difficult decisions in coaching is whether to push or back off—whether to use a pat on the back or a kick in the butt.

In general, it is important that the person gets out there and exercises regularly with some enjoyment from each session. When motivation is down, just shoot for a minimal amount, every other day. Realize, however, that to really get hooked, the new walker must develop the desire from within.

Rewards definitely do work!

After a certain number of weeks, or after reaching a certain level of fitness, surprise with a reward. It doesn't have to be something expensive or exotic. The reward allows the new exerciser to focus on his or her progress, and feel the satisfaction of steady work paying off.

Find a fun race to attend

Races are such positive experiences for new walkers, when they have a good leader to coach them through the experience: calming the anxieties and sharing the celebration. Your new exerciser will almost always realize that he or she is like most of the others in the race. Just having a race date on a calendar will provide the beginner with an identity that will increase motivation.

Admit your own mistakes

When you open up to your novice with a personal story, the lessons become more powerful.

Don't over-sell the positives

The benefits are so powerful that almost everyone who stays with it for 6 months will continue. If your coachee is falling asleep during your one hour speech on the wonderful world of cardiovascular fitness, you know that you've stepped over the line. The experience is more powerful than the preaching—and both are part of the process.

An independent exerciser—your ultimate reward

Take it as a real compliment that your coachee will need less and less of your guidance. This means that you were an excellent coach, and that he or she can find a new person and enrich another life—and you can too.

So how long do the benefits continue?

Most walkers who stay focused, continue to improve their endurance and overall fitness for at least 10 years. Some will move on to running and see significant improvements in speed and distance. While the satisfaction comes mostly from the effect of each individual exercise session, you will have many options.

Even if you get caught up in time improvement, I suggest that you find several areas of exercise enjoyment which can continue to enrich your life. You can select events in every state, each continent, every country in Europe, etc. Have several reunions with your growing number of exercise friends, 2-4 times a year. Have a family challenge and meet in a city where most of the family wants to visit.

The best form of walking improvement comes from inside. My faster times are long gone, but I enjoy my exercise and appreciate it now more than ever. Practically every day I feel better, work better, think better because I cover my miles. It doesn't get any better!

Heart disease and walking

Walking tends to have a protective effect from cardiovascular disease. But more walkers die of heart disease than any other cause, and are susceptible to the same risk factors as sedentary people. I know of a number of long term exercisers who have suffered heart attacks and strokes who, according to the experts, could have prevented them if they had taken a few simple tests.

Your heart is the most important organ in your body. This short section is offered as a guide to help you take charge over your heart health—the most important organ for longevity, and quality of life. As always, you need to get advice about your individual situation from a cardiologist who knows you and specializes in this area. It is always a good idea to get tested, even if you are in your 30s, to use as baseline data.

Risk Factors—get checked if you have two of these—or one that is serious (especially the first)

- Family history of cardiovascular disease or diabetes
- Poor lifestyle habits earlier in life
- High fat/high cholesterol diet
- Have smoked—or still smoke
- Obese or severely overweight
- High blood pressure
- High cholesterol

Tests

- Stress test—heart is monitored during a walk that gradually increases in difficulty.
- C reactive protein—has been an indicator of increased risk.
- Heart scan—an electronic scan of the heart which shows calcification, and possible narrowing of arteries.
- Radioactive dye test—very effective in locating specific blockages. Talk to your doctor about this.

None of these are fool proof. But by working with your cardiologist, you can increase your chance of living until the muscles just won't propel you further down the road—past the age of 100.

LEARNING TO RUN

Many of today's runners started as walkers. Some walked for a decade or two before taking their first running steps. This is a sample section—try it out a bit to see if you like it. My Run-Walk-Run™ method allows you to control the way you feel when you run, as you alternate running and walking.

Is running better than walking?

Walking is a great exercise that produces few injuries, while burning calories and building fitness. Once conditioned to recreational walking, one can burn many calories without realizing it. The purpose of this section is not to get walkers to switch to running—but to provide a gentle challenge to those who want a bit more exertion than is provided by walking. A significant percentage of walkers incorporate some running into their exercise, after 6-12 months.

The evolution of a runner
- At first, the walk was a bit of a challenge to the sedentary body.
- Each walk delivered some exertion-related relaxation and inner satisfaction.
- But after several weeks or months of regular walking, the walker's improved fitness level reduced the post-walk rewards.
- The walker inserts a few short runs into the daily walks
- The run segments became more frequent.
- After the run-walk-run days, the walker felt better than he/she did after the walk-only days.
- The walker alternates between running and walking, as desired.

Reasons given for running

Many walkers start running because they need to squeeze their exercise into a smaller block of time. Often this results from seeing a former sedentary neighbor (co-worker, family member, etc.) who was wearing a running T-shirt, or who was running through the neighborhood. The list of benefits from an individual will vary widely. Since I hear them every day from satisfied running "customers" the following are some of the most common:

Top reasons that walkers switch to running

1. Running burns twice as many calories as walking the same distance.
2. Running delivers a unique sense of relaxation.
3. Running controls fat much more effectively.
4. Running leaves one with an enhanced attitude to face the rest of the day.
5. Running burns the same number of calories in about 50% of the time, or less.
6. Running leaves one with a better dose of sustained physical energy.
7. Running bestows a greater sense of accomplishment.
8. Running gives one a sense of freedom not delivered by other activities.

As you begin to run, you will discover a wide range of positive feelings and experiences from body, mind and spirit. This is your body's way of overcoming the challenges of fatigue, aches, pains, and mental doubt. As you deal with each of these, you tie into the internal strengths that have been part of the human condition from the origin of the species. The result of this "gearing up" is an afterglow. A common reaction is that the run cleanses the mind. The rewards just keep on coming and there are few internal feelings more powerful or more directly connected to our being than those that come from running.

Run-Walk-Run™ method

In 1973 I was asked to teach a class on beginning running. Since none of those enrolled had been doing any consistent running I designed a method similar to the "shuffle breaks" described in this book. At first, short run segments were inserted into the walk. Gradually, the running segments increased and the walking time decreased. By the end of the class every one of the members completed a 5K or a 10K, injury-free.

By gradually introducing your body to running, you can see if you like it. The key is to stay on the conservative side. With this method you determine how much running you will do. You will never have to run continuously.

A short, gentle stride

Run with a very relaxed, short stride that feels comfortable: feet low to the ground, lightly touching. Don't lift your knees. In general, make it easy on yourself. For more suggestions on easier running, see my book *Running: Getting Started*.

The first run

After you have been walking for several months, and have increased to walking for at least 30 minutes, you can try this out during one of your short walks during the week. The key is to do only a few seconds of running at first. Here is how it works:

1. Walk for at least 3 minutes at a slow walk to warm the muscles up gently

2. For 2 more minutes, continue to walk slowly, or increase to a normal walk pace if you wish.

3. Then alternate segments of 5-10 seconds of running (no more) with 1-2 minutes of comfortable walking

4. Do this for 5-10 minutes—no more

5. Walk slowly for the remaining time of your walk as a "warm down"

6. If you liked this, then here is a sample program to try:

Your "Introduction to Running Program"

Mon	Tue	Wed	Thu	Fri	Sat	Sun

Week 1—run 5-10 seconds/walk 1-2 minutes

Mon	Tue	Wed	Thu	Fri	Sat	Sun
20-30 min Run-Walk	walk 30 min or off	20-30 min Run-Walk	walk 30 min or off	off	Long Walk (no running)	30 min Walk

Week 2—run 5-15 seconds/walk 1-2 minutes

Mon	Tue	Wed	Thu	Fri	Sat	Sun
20-30 min Run-Walk	walk 30 min or off	20-30 min Run-Walk	walk 30 min or off	off	Long Walk (no running)	30 min Walk

Week 3—run 10-15 seconds/walk 1-2 minutes

Mon	Tue	Wed	Thu	Fri	Sat	Sun
20-30 min Run-Walk	walk 25 min or off	20-30 min Run-walk	walk 25 min or off	off	Long Walk (no running)	30 min Walk

Week 4—run 10-20 seconds/walk 1-2 min

Mon	Tue	Wed	Thu	Fri	Sat	Sun
20-30 min Run-Walk	walk 30 min or off	20-30 min Run-Walk	walk 30 min or off	off	Long Walk (no running)	30 min Walk

Week 5—run 10-20 seconds/walk 1-2 min

Mon	Tue	Wed	Thu	Fri	Sat	Sun
20-30 min 30 min Run-Walk	walk or off	20-30 min Run-Walk	walk 30 min or off	off	Long Walk (no running)	30 min Walk

Note:
For the complete beginning running program, see *Running: Getting Started* (www.JeffGallo way.com)

ROSWELL REGIONAL LIBRARY

Photo Credits

Cover Design: Jens Vogelsang

Cover Photo: jump photo agency

Back Cover: Polar Electro
Andy Sharp

Inside Photos: Polar Electro
Andy Sharp
imsi GmbH